Doing Business
with China

Paul Leppert

Jain Publishing Company
Fremont, California

The purpose of this book is to provide helpful information to people doing business with Asians. It is sold with the understanding that it is not designed to render legal, accounting, or other professional advice. For such services contact a competent practitioner.

Library of Congress Cataloguing-in-Publication Data

Leppert, Paul A.
    Doing business with China / Paul Leppert.
       p.   cm.
    Includes bibliographical references and index.
    ISBN 0-87573-045-0
      1. China--Commerce--United States--Handbooks, manuals, etc.
    2. United States--Commerce--China--Handbooks, manuals, etc.
    3. China--Description and travel.   I. Title.
HF3838.U6L47   1994
650'.0951--dc20

                                                  94-9350
                                                   CIP

Contents

Introduction

This book is written for American business people who plan to do business with citizens of the People's Republic of China. It is designed to help those who have not previously dealt with the Chinese people overcome anxiety and engage in cross-cultural business more effectively.

China's population is over a billion. Its annual population growth exceeds the number of Texans. China has huge untapped resources. Greater China, consisting of the People's Republic of China, Hong Kong, and Taiwan probably has more economic and business potential than Japan. Some economists project China to be the leading world commercial power by the early twenty-first century. Businesses with global ambitions must not ignore it.

In anticipation of the 1997 reversion of Hong Kong to China this is the first book of its kind to integrate Hong Kong into the Chinese business environment. The topic of doing business in two other countries with Chinese culture, Taiwan and Singapore, is covered by other books in this series: *Doing Business with the Chinese: Taiwan* and *Doing Business in Singapore*.

This book, like the others in the series, follows a common pattern: a description of cultural patterns, an explanation of how these are passed to children by the family, an analysis of how such cultural conditioning affects business behavior, and suggestions on how an American business person can use this knowledge. Additional material concerns how to enjoy China and its people.

The culture of China is difficult to analyze because it is in a state of flux. The Confucian ethic which prevailed in China for twenty-five centuries was challenged by communist concepts which have failed but left indelible effects. Things in China will never be quite the same. Recent events leave Westerners in wonder. Many Chinese are equally perplexed. They see a China progressing from Confucius to confusion. The West had hundreds of years to digest many revolutions; China is trying to absorb them all at once. The outcome is difficult to predict. We can glimpse the vague shape of a new greater China but cannot visualize its exact contours.

The first part of this book describes cultural and social factors which affect doing business in China. Culture, a product of history, is passed from generation to generation by such institutions as the family, the school, and the temple. The business behavior of your Chinese counterpart will be profoundly affected by the culture he or she learned as a child. To do business with Chinese you must learn how Chinese culture affects Chinese behavior.

The second part of this book deals with the economic and business environment in China. It explains how the Chinese economy and business system originated and developed and describes its successes, opportunities, problems, and pitfalls. Of particular interest are China's business procedures, bargaining techniques, and sources of help. These too, are rooted in culture.

The third and final section is concerned with your personal experience with China: travel tips; things to do, see, and learn; living conditions, useful addresses, and recommended reading. This section will help you adjust to China, particularly if you were not too excited about going there!

This book is based partly on interviews with Chinese and American business people and officials of government. It is designed to get you started. It does not intend to provide legal advice or solutions to specific business problems which vary widely. Conditions in China are constantly changing. There are new regulations almost daily. Although every effort has been made to ensure accuracy there are always exceptions such as local rules and alternative procedures. Much will depend on how well you bargain. Be sure to check with the offices and agencies listed in chapters nine and thirteen for the latest information before making business decisions. More detailed information can be found in the books listed in chapter fourteen.

The information provided here does not represent the views of any agencies of the People's Republic of China or the United States. Money is denominated in U.S. dollars unless otherwise specified.

PART ONE

Knowing Your Counterpart

Culture is not a house one can enter and leave at will. So powerful is its conditioning that it defines thought, determines behavior, and limits expression. Though it embraces the full gamut of human activity from business to the arts, it sets silent parameters as stringently as an electric fence. Within its grasp we are all Pavlovian dogs.

Chinese business people have different goals and procedures because their culture espouses different values. Before you begin your business dealings with Chinese, you will want to learn everything you can about them. How do these people view themselves, their families, work, culture and politics? Their attitudes toward these have a profound effect on the way they do business.

Childhood cultural imprinting, because it is subconscious, has a powerful and insidious effect on adult behavior. When people from different cultures do business, each behaves according to cultural patterns learned in childhood. If you understand your counterpart's cultural conditioning, you will have a decided advantage.

1. Culture and Society

The Land

China's culture, like all others, was conditioned by the land which nurtured it. A large, disparate resource-rich physical setting produced a large, disparate, self-sufficient society. The land was the stage; the people, the cast. Together they produced one of the world's greatest dramas.

China's complicated crosshatch of mountain ranges created a checkerboard of valleys and plains which impeded economic and political unity. Even in recent times a variety of warlords and economic czars flaunted the central government. Fortunately some of the mountains provided watersheds for mighty rivers, such as the Yangze and Xi, which were plied by junks and sampans from the earliest times. Rivers provided water and silt for agriculture, particularly rice. A variety of climates produced a variety of crops. Great forests yielded wood for heating, cooking, and construction. Coal was burned so early that Marco Polo's account of Chinese use of this magical rock was beyond belief of Europeans. In later years China's ample reserves of crude oil, natural gas, tungsten, coal, iron, antimony, copper, gold, titanium, tin, lead, and zinc would provide a potential for substantial economic development.

The land of the dragons was both blessed and victimized by geography. Isolated by the world's highest mountains, largest ocean, and driest deserts, China established a high culture and a towering ego. Behind this curtain of isolation a unique and glorious civilization arose and flowered.

In time, due partly to lack of challenge and stimulation from outside, it stagnated and declined. Through it all the Chinese viewed their culture as superior and called their country "the Middle Kingdom." All foreigners were considered barbarians.

The climate, dominated by the monsoon, the heartbeat of Asia, could be both benevolent and brutal. In the winter cold dry air settles over Siberia and Manchuria. It blows southward, creating dust storms in the north. When it meets warmer, wet air in the south it produces rain. In the summer and autumn the monsoon brings wet tropical storms from the Pacific and Indian oceans. These are simultaneously supplemented by typhoons, the hurricanes of the Pacific, which batter the China coast with torrential rains and destructive winds. Such cyclic extremes produce death by drought and disease, disastrous floods and famines, clouds of locusts and other unpleasant scourges. Millions of Chinese have perished in some of these disasters. At the dawn of Chinese civilization the institution of the emperor was established partly to placate nature's heaven with sufficient ceremony and sacrifice to prevent such catastrophes.

Nevertheless natural calamities occurred on such an overwhelming scale and with such frequency that emperors lost their thrones and China developed philosophies such as Taoism and Confucianism which stressed adjustment to the vagaries of nature. Unlike Westerners who tried to conquer it, Chinese tried to accept nature and join it. This concept is reflected in Chinese paintings which are dominated by magnificent mountains, billowing clouds, and bursting blossoms. One must strain to find a human figure represented as a distant dot merging with nature.

China's experience with the great cycles of nature produced a concept of time much different from the West's. The Chinese view of time is cyclical not linear. Time bends back on itself distorting the differences between past, present, and future. Chinese often look at their history with a view unsullied by the turbulent currents of time. When a Western reporter asked a Chinese official how things were going in China *now*, he answered by describing problems at the start of the Ming Dynasty, more than four hundred years prior to the French Revolution!

Business and Culture

Your business activities can benefit in many ways from a knowledge of Chinese culture. It will help you understand and anticipate the behavior of your Chinese business counterpart. Chinese culture is easier for an outsider to understand than American culture because Chinese culture is less diverse and Chinese are bound to it more tightly. You are fortunate that Chinese are predictable not inscrutable.

Your knowledge of Chinese culture will guide you in proper etiquette, win respect from Chinese associates, and help you enjoy Chinese festivals, literature, arts, music and cuisine. An awareness of Chinese styles of non-verbal communication and a rudimentary familiarity with Mandarin can enhance your business communication.

Foundations of Chinese Culture

Chinese culture has survived more centuries and influenced more human beings than any other. It was fully flowering when Europe was still in the throes of savagery. So tightly does this culture cleave to the bedrock of history that China's tumultuous twentieth century revolutions could not uproot it. Its fruits include conformity with nature, stress on stability, and strong group cohesion.

The Chinese acceptance of nature has many social implications. One is the assumption that the group is more important than the individual. Nature's only concern for the single organism is to encourage its survival until it procreates. In some species thousands are born from one sexual union. Only a few survive. Millions die daily. For Chinese "rights" belong to groups or species not individuals. This precept of natural order conditions Chinese culture, law, and business. Confucius taught that "the nail which sticks up is hammered down." Only the group has "freedom." Such a concept is in marked contrast to the exaltation of the individual in Western culture which assumes that great diversity of personal attributes will benefit society. President Wilson once summarized this view: "There is no such thing as corporate freedom. Freedom belongs to the individual or it does not exist." There is great contrast between the Chinese social system of mutual obligations and the American stress on individual rights.

Acceptance of nature also implies a secular view of life which is reflected in Chinese philosophy. Neither Confucianism nor Taoism is a religion. Their founders refused to speculate on the supernatural or an afterlife. Confucianism is an ethical system concerned with relationships between people. Taoism is a philosophical system concerned with a person's relationship with a mysterious inner self. Both stress harmony with nature.

The Chinese are possibly the only people in the world who did not originate a religion. Islam, Buddhism, and Christianity were imported to Chinese who felt no compunction at practicing religions part-time or simultaneously, buffet style. One can find a pantheon of minor spirits, kitchen gods, and wood nymphs but indigenous Chinese religion was never well developed, organized, or institutionalized. The atheism of communism was not a reason for its rejection in China. Unlike Jews and Moslems (who are denied pork) and Hindus (who are denied beef) the Chinese have no religious food taboos. These omnivores enjoy the world's most varied cuisine: dog, cat, snake, sea slug, fish brains, rat dumplings, and swallows nest soup consisting of the birds' gluey spit. In the wok of the world's best cooks even road splat can be a delicacy.

For Chinese the hierarchy of nature must be reflected in social inequality. All people are created *unequal* and remain so, not just in family and work roles, but in their intrinsic worth. Confucius taught a system of inequality based on conformity to a system of rights and obligations between superiors and inferiors. This acceptance of inequality helps explain why the communist system failed in China and why your Chinese business counterpart will feel comfortable as your superior or inferior but never as your equal.

Hierarchy can only exist in groups. Chinese seek security by conforming to the values and status ladders of the family, clan, work unit, or business. Only through cohesion to the group can one find shelter from the vicissitudes of life. Americans may ask a stranger "Who are you?" Chinese ask "*Ni Nar?*" meaning "Where are you? What is your group?"

The traditional Chinese group was the clan which likely evolved from early tribes. It produced the *xing* or family name. Even today people with the same family names (perhaps the Chinese equivalent of Smith) do not marry, even though there is no blood relationship. Reverence for ancestors probably developed to encourage clan cohesion.

China under communism replaced the clan with the *dan hui* (work unit) which chooses and provides housing, utilities, health care, food, nurseries, transportation, retirement, and ration books for its members. *Dan hui* permission is needed to marry, have children (one per couple) and travel. Some hotels and restaurants will only accept reservations from work units not individuals. If a member commits a crime the entire unit might suffer. This system of group responsibility has been described as a type of modern feudalism.

The work unit is now being replaced by business entities similar to those which have long existed in Singapore, Hong Kong, and Taiwan. These are not as stringent or intrusive as the work unit but they still tie down their members in such a crosshatch of obligations that they end up like the giant in *Gulliver's Travels*, unable to move.

Philosophy and Religion

Both Taoism and Confucianism stress harmony and achievement by living within the rules of nature.

Though Confucius was not the only influence on Chinese culture he had more impact than Jesus on the West. Confucian concepts such as respect for authority, ancestors, education, and family survived China's twentieth century revolutions. Confucius, born 551 B.C., systematized and promoted a concept of human relationships during a time of troubles. His teaching involved obligations between unequals: father and son, husband and wife, older and younger brothers, ruler and subject, nature/heaven and monarch. When a ruler failed to perform the rites to heaven exactly as prescribed he lost its mandate. Ensuing famines, floods, droughts, disease, rebellions, and war would show heaven's displeasure with the monarch and justify his removal. No elections were needed.

The philosophy of Taoism founded by Lao-tse in the sixth century B.C. stresses meditation and intuition. "Tao" means "the way," a concept which defies definition. It approximates the unseen energy of nature, the ground of being, the source of life, both within one and in nature.

Though the Chinese are very worldly, pragmatic and secular, some religions were imported to satisfy needs not served by Confucianism and Taoism. Since the reduction of Buddhist power in the Tang Dynasty, religion has not been a major force in China. The current Chinese constitution does not outlaw the practice of religion, just preaching it. Even this restriction is loosening in practice.

Buddhism entered China from India where it was founded by Siddhartha Gautama, the Buddha, born 503 B.C. Buddhism which has no god began as a protest against Hinduism which has many. Like most Eastern religions Buddhism seeks salvation by accepting nature and merging the soul into it. In contrast Christianity seeks salvation by transcending nature and saving the soul. Compared to Western religions which tend to control the daily lives of its adherents, Buddhism has great tolerance. Buddha defined life as suffering. One could end the cycle of reincarnation and achieve the pleasant nothingness of nirvana only by conquering all desire and surrendering the ego of individuality. Kuan Yin, the Buddhist goddess of mercy, takes a role similar to Mother Mary in Christianity. Chinese are more likely to be guided by Confucius in their everyday lives and turn to Buddhism at times of birth, old age, sickness, and death.

Islam was founded by the prophet Muhammad in Arabia in the seventh century, A.D. and entered China with traders from the Middle East. Islam enters every facet of its adherents' lives through a strict code called *Sharia*. In China Islam lost some of its compulsive passion. Most Chinese Moslems live in the western provinces. Chinese bearing the family name of "Ma" are likely to be Mohammedans.

Christian missionaries have been active in China for many years. Chinese who convert to Christianity to gain advantages of Western education or medicine are called "rice Christians." There are substantial numbers of Chinese Christians in the old treaty ports such as Shanghai and Canton.

The Chinese are eclectic about religion. If it is good to accept one religion, why not all? A variety of beliefs are incorporated into amorphous and syncretic popular religions involving omens, kitchen and village gods, lucky talismans and other superstitions.

Festivals and Holidays

Traditions regarding festivals and holidays are in flux. With looser communist cultural controls traditional holidays are more popular. It is not likely that the birthday of the British queen will be celebrated after Hong Kong's return to China. Chinese employees expect considerable time off for festivals and holidays; for lunar New Year's, big bonuses.

National holidays in China include New Year's Day, 1 January; International Working Women's Day, 8 March; Labor Day, 1 May; Youth Day, 4 May; Children's Day, 1 June;

Birthday of Chinese Communist Party, 1 July; People's Liberation Army Day, 1 August, and National Day, 1 October.

Hong Kong's holidays include New Year's Day, 1 January; the Easter holidays; Buddha's birthday and Bun Festival in May; Dragon Boat Festival in May or June; and the queen's birthday in June.

Cultural holidays common to all Chinese include the lunar New Year, held on the first day of the first moon, usually late January or February. Stores and offices close. Lodging and transportation are packed with people returning to their ancestral homes. Chinese start anew: cleaning houses, paying debts, and visiting relatives.

Painting

Chinese painting reflects nature as conceived, not perceived by the painter. By the Song Dynasty subjects had centered on the brief and fragile beauty of birds and flowers and the eternal immensity of mountains. Landscapes included tiny human figures to instill perspective and humility: big nature, small man, including the viewer. Xu Beihong and Qi Baishi, early twentieth century artists revived the art of brush painting in broad bold strokes. I enjoyed Xu's brilliant creations at the Shanghai Museum.

In dynastic days paintings were too fragile to hang on walls. They were rendered on handscrolls, conserved in camphor cases, opened and unrolled only for guests.

Calligraphy

Calligraphy, brush painting of Chinese characters, one of the highest Asian art forms, is little esteemed by Westerners. Appreciation requires a knowledge of Chinese characters because the essence of calligraphy is the rendering of strokes in ways which emphasize their meanings: bold for a strong idea, uncertain for a shy one, dripping for a tearful event. Try it in English!

Architecture

Early Chinese architects designed buildings to be integral parts of the landscape. The art of *feng shui* ensured buildings were in harmony with nature. Most temples, palaces, and houses were "U" shaped with open courtyards facing south to provide sun and shelter from winter winds.

By the early Tang period roofs already had uplifts at the corners and ceramic monsters meant to fight fires and frighten foreigners. Examples may be viewed in the Forbidden City in Beijing.

Handicrafts

A visit to a Chinese museum will quickly impress one with the exquisite taste and painstaking expertise involved in the creation of this culture's art. The best porcelain is flawless and translucent. Its glaze is fused in such fervid fires that it responds with a clear musical note when struck. Though both porcelain and silk were exported in vast quantities, China kept their production processes secret for thousands of years.

Each dynasty produced its own distinct porcelain. The Tang palette of glazes featured flashes of iridescent blue, yellow and green. The Southern Song produced matchless blue-green celadons using iron oxide glazes. By the time of the Mongols mass production for a mass market resulted in declines in quality. Their blue and white porcelain flooded the Middle East. Soon "chintzy" defined cheap and shoddy Chinese goods.

Lacquerware began in southern China when the sap of the sumac was used to preserve furniture in the hot, moist climate. Chinese cast fine bronzes as early as 1600 B.C. Shang Dynasty food and ceremonial bowls mysteriously appeared as fully developed art objects, suggesting origins elsewhere.

Bronzes used to offer food to the gods were buried with the owner so the deceased could continue the ritual. By the time of Confucius this practice was considered an unwise waste and bronzes were used for mirrors and flower vases for the living.

Language

Mandarin as spoken in Beijing is the official language. It has little grammar and most sounds are similar to English. Meaning is based on four tone inflections. Depending on the tone used "ma" means mother, hemp, horse, or scold. With the help of tapes or a tutor you can learn sufficient phrases to ease your visit.

The various forms of spoken Chinese are not dialects but languages because they are mutually unintelligible. Phonetic romanizations of the various languages are also mutually unintelligible. Yet all of these spoken languages share the same written language which is expressed in characters which have the same meaning for all but are pronounced differently. One can see Chinese who speak different spoken languages write the common characters on paper to communicate. If all Chinese became fluent in Mandarin its romanization might be used instead of characters. This goal has not been attained.

Parts of each character sometimes give clues to its pronunciation and meaning but usually they do not. Since there is no alphabet a student of the language must memorize the writing, meaning, and pronunciation of each, one by one. About five thousand characters are needed for basic communication.

Mandarin has several romanizations. The Wade-Giles system was created in the nineteenth century, the Yale system was developed in the 1940s, and pinyin originated in China in the late 1950s. This book uses pinyin except where usage of another romanization is so entrenched that it would confuse the reader. In pinyin Lao-tse, the philosopher, is Lao zi.

Literature and Drama

Much of Chinese culture is based on the five Confucian classics: *Book of Poetry, Book of History, Book of Changes (I Ching), Spring and Autumn Annals,* and the *Book of Rites.* The four great books are the *Analects, Book of Mencius, Book of Great Learning,* and *Doctrine of the Mean.*

The Romance of the Three Kingdoms describes great rebellions after the Later Han Dynasty. This tale is the origin of Mao's statement: "To rebel is justified!" Other famous books include *All Men Are Brothers,* a story about a band like Robin Hood's; *Dream of the Red Chamber;* and *Monkey.*

Lu Xun's writings highlighted Chinese literature in the 1920s. During the Cultural Revolution literature, like the other arts, was required to express a socialist point of view. Today expression is freer. Insights into modern Chinese life are revealed by GuHua's *A Small Town Called Hibiscus,* Jiang Zilong's *All the Colors of the Rainbow,* and Liu Shaotang's *Catkin Willow Flats.*

China's two great lyric poets, Li Po and Tu Fu, lived in the eighth century. They loved nature. Li Po overdid it, became drunk and drowned leaning too far out of a boat as he tried to kiss the moon.

China's colorful opera which first appeared in the Mongol Dynasty is back. It features acrobatics, high-pitched monologues, and symbolic gestures. A warrior mounts a horse by raising a leg and dismounts by throwing his riding whip on the floor. Flags moved in waves mean storm at sea.

Unlike Western audiences, Chinese refuse to be intimidated by actors. They display disdain by shouting coarse comments. Screaming tots run up and down the aisles. Adults spit bones and pumpkin seeds on the floor. Inept performers are laughed off the stage. In spite of the noise the show goes on. The clamor of the band conquers all.

Cultural and Social Change

For China the changes of the twentieth century have been cataclysmic. In the waning years of the last dynasty the Chinese could look back at thousands of years of usually stable imperial rule based on Confucian values. But deep down the tectonic plates were shifting. A series of violent cultural tremors and social upheavals would soon crack the foundations of the great tradition and shift leadership from ruling gentry to revolutionary guards. The aftershocks continue today.

China's weakness before Western economic and military pressure forced reforms which culminated in the Cultural Revolution and transformed society by encouraging the young to attack the old. Schools were closed, temples and museums destroyed, books burned. Millions had their houses sacked, suffered torture and were exiled to distant rural areas to do hard labor simply because they had educations or skills which set them apart from the masses. Many of these were forced to live in pigpens, which in Chinese farmhouses are located under privies so pigs can eat the human feces which fall from above. The Cultural Revolution in its passion for equality abolished workers' bonuses, private plots, and free markets. It was the ultimate victory over the individual and it failed miserably. Fortunately in the long sweep of Chinese history it will be but a brief darkness at noon.

Though the communist eclipse is over, the modern age brings its own dark shadows: mass migrations, corruption, pollution, crime, social discord, traffic congestion. Millions of rural Chinese move to the cities in the hope of finding industrial work. Those finding none either enter an urban underworld or sign with syndicates, pledging years of work as indentured servants to pay for hazardous voyages and illegal entries into the United States.

China is entering a modern world culture which is itself confused. It moves with dizzying speed from agriculture to information technology, from religious mass to mass production, from delayed gratification to conspicuous consumption. Its shape is amorphous and it leaves a trail of oxymorons: socially impotent power structures, industrial success which ruins the environment, and wasteful creativity. The visions and values needed to guide behavior blur. So some individuals follow the whims of the moment applauding change as their cultures dissolve.

With economic success the Chinese, like the West, might drift in the currents of social change. When storms bring high winds which rip the sails, they might lack a dependable doctrinal anchor.

risk

Yet it is possible that China's cultural heritage will bring it some special advantages: the ability to live close together with less rancor than most societies, respect for learning, and an admirable work ethic.

As the veneer of communism rubs off the underlying Confucian structure, though exhibiting some dry rot, retains sufficient strength to support newer social structures. In 1974 China's communist government launched a major campaign against the 2500 year old system of Confucianism. That this was necessary after more than a generation of communist ideological inculcation testifies to the tenacity of this ancient tradition.

2. Family Life

Family Structure

Sun Yat-sen once described the Chinese as a million grains of sand (each a family) with nothing to hold them together (as a nation). In spite of revolutionary efforts to modify it, the family is still the most important institution in China. When introduced Chinese give family names first. Be sure to ask about your Chinese counterpart's family.

A member of a Chinese family does not do his or her "own thing." The good of the family comes first. It is considered an act of selfishness for one to make decisions without family approval. Such obligations produce considerable tensions but Chinese are willing to bear them because the family functions as both a provider and shelter from the storms of life.

Safe haven does not extend to female fetuses. Chinese couples often have the sex of an unborn child checked with ultrasound scanners. With a ratio of one hundred and twenty boys born for every hundred girls China's huge population aborts almost two million female fetuses per year. Since couples are limited to one child they make sure it is male. This is a new version of the traditional practice of female infanticide.

Early Childhood

Young children participate in most family activities and enjoy great freedom. Upbringing is very different than in the

West. Chinese strive to make a child dependent on the family; Americans want self-reliant children. Chinese help a baby up after it has fallen; Americans may let it pull itself up. Chinese children sleep in the same room as their parents; American kids have their own. An American child who is "bad" may not be allowed out of the house; a Chinese couple will *put* a naughty child out.

Chinese families live as units. At meals food is taken from family serving dishes, a bit at a time. Babies attend restaurants with parents. Because they are seldom alone, Chinese find Western ideas of privacy strange.

The dependence of children on their families makes it easier to indoctrinate them with cultural values such as respect for parents, obedience, patience, and social harmony. The young child learns about "face" and shame. "Face" is a type of personal dignity. It is achieved by avoiding confrontation and open display of emotion. Losing "face" brings humiliation. The young child will learn to feel shame when failing to meet the expectations of the group. But it will never experience guilt, which is reserved for masochistic Westerners who punish themselves when only their consciences know of their transgressions.

The Chinese Home

Your counterpart will likely invite you to a restaurant since most Chinese homes are small and lack conveniences found in American homes.

If you *are* invited to a Chinese home be sure to remove your shoes at the entrance and ask to be invited inside. Always bring a gift such as flowers or sweets. Offer it with both hands. Your host will open it when alone.

During meals the wife will spend most of the time in the kitchen since dishes are served one after another. Do not appeal to her to join you because that is the Chinese way. The host will probably put food on your plate. When finished leave a little food on your plate to show you had enough.

Education

Mandatory education is being extended from the traditional six years. Many Chinese do not graduate from high school. Fewer attend one of roughly five hundred universities. Nevertheless the literacy rate is about eighty-five per cent and rising.

Chinese education does not teach students to "find" themselves. Instead it teaches good citizenship through conformity and discipline. Moral, political, and social values are taught as well as academic subjects.

Sometimes the goal of producing a good citizen fails and a child grows up to be a criminal. Even then the idea of conformity to a group (in this case a gang) remains. Chinese convenience stores are never held up by lone gunmen.

Adolescence

A child reaching adolescence finds it difficult to deviate from prescribed social standards because the teaching of the schools is buttressed by media controls which allow no alternative role models. A Chinese child who stays home "sick" from school to watch television has a choice of English or algebra lessons or Mandarin morality plays. Chinese children do not commit violence due to conduct observed on television, videos, or in movies.

By adolescence a young person will have several strong friendships with schoolmates. Many of these will grow into adult business or professional relationships which will be valued over others.

Courtship and Marriage

During the revolutionary period the government version of romance involved a boy, a girl, and a tractor. Although the tractor has now lost out, required government approval to marry comes at a late age, about thirty for men and twenty-five for women.

Although marriages are no longer arranged they are manipulated. Families will often get their marriagable off-spring together with the hope romance will develop. Soon the young couples are making every effort to win over each other's family.

Weddings were quick and simple during the revolution-ary period. Now some are more decorous with much feasting and laughter. If you are invited to one it is good to bring a gift of money in even bills, packed in a red envelope.

Work

Most workers, particularly those in industry, work forty-four hour, five-and-a-half day weeks and take seven public holidays. The government has separate pay scales for factory workers, engineers, technicians, and bureaucrats. The private sector is required to meet certain minimum wage require-ments. Unions are required for foreign firms.

Since a 1985 reform there have been more incentives. These may be based on profitability of the enterprise, quality of individual work, or skills.

The Chinese government has wisely allowed private businesses to slowly replace government companies rather than closing or selling state enterprises as in Eastern Europe. This has avoided considerable unemployment and provided for a smoother transition.

In a typical Chinese family both parents will work. Some will check in at a government job and immediately leave for another in the private sector. For this reason both the size of the economy and personal income are understated.

Chinese work long hours but do not seem as rushed or driven as Americans. As in America one's work tends to deter-mine one's status in society, but the workplace of Chinese has a much more powerful influence on their everyday lives.

Recreation

The Chinese have a lively sense of humor and a zest for life. They particularly enjoy sports, travel, and public performances.

The most popular sports are soccer, swimming, basketball, and table tennis. Ballets, operas, theaters, and movies entertain large audiences. Tai chi, a shadow boxing routine, and Chinese chess are very popular.

With rising incomes many Chinese are seeing their country for the first time. First class travel used to be the privilege of Westerners and bureaucrats. But now many Chinese have the affluence to travel this way.

Recreation is usually a family activity. Since living quarters are sparse and tight, family picnics and outings are very popular.

Old Age and Death

Old age arrives late in China. The heroes of Chinese literature are often portrayed with gray hair. Though their faces are wrinkled, their personalities have been smoothed by time like fine jade. Many of China's political leaders are in their eighties and nineties.

Very old people retain their importance in the family long after they are unable to participate in work or decisions. Often they watch the house or take care of small children while working members are away. In return their families take care of them. In China it is a criminal offense not to support elderly parents.

When visiting a Chinese family be sure to defer to older members.

The government encourages cremation but families are free to commemorate death as they wish. Some include a wake and a parade involving a brass band and blown up photos of the deceased. As in the West a death in the family brings social unity. Members of the extended family return home.

Change

There have been several recent studies concerning the extent of damage caused the family in the revolutionary period. All conclude the family survived with considerable strength and integrity.

But the stamina of the family as an institution does not preclude change in values. While Chinese still accept the roles of benevolent fathers and filial sons and prefer male offspring to female, they now want to raise children, including daughters, who are more assertive. Traditional Chinese values relegated merchants to the bottom of society but a business career is now considered a worthy goal for a child.

Family members are less willing to "live in harmony" when they disagree with the goals of the chief harmonizer. The Chinese family and its members now want a degree of economic and political power which may well conflict with the scenarios of China's power elite.

Though values may change the Chinese family will always be held responsible for the people it produces. This is emphasized by the grim tradition which requires a family to pay for the bullet fired into the back of the head of a member executed as a criminal.

3. Politics and Law

Origins

The five thousand year sprawl of Chinese politics must be fathomed to understand modern China. For here, more than anywhere else, the past explains the present. The crush of tanks in Tiananmen Square in June 1989, affirmed a long tradition of willing acceptance of a tyrannical authority tolerating no dissent.

Cultures create and carry only the political systems people desire and deserve. From the days of the legendary Fu Xi to Deng Hsiaoping Chinese authoritarianism has been publicly supported with great alacrity. For its willing subjects China's autocracy has produced longer periods of peace and prosperity for more people than any other in world history.

Individuals were willing to harbor hidden hatred and feign indifference to official contumely because order was too highly valued to be risked by foolhardy experiments with pluralism or civil rights. Only when tyranny became unbearably blatant did society erupt with violence. Even then the upheavals which ended dynasties were not directed against the system but the leaders who could not run it properly.

Imperial Period

The Chinese system of dynasties began millennia ago with the rise of petty kingdoms near the great bend in the Yellow River. The founder of a ruling house was usually a strong man who took over in a time of troubles. Emperors who kept the irrigation dikes in repair, properly performed the rites to heaven, and warded off invasions, famine, corruption, drought and disease kept the mandate of heaven and their thrones. Those who failed these tasks were replaced by coups, riots, assassinations and other unpleasant political surprises. Revolts were led by such colorful bands as the Red Eyebrows, Five Pecks of Rice, Yellow Turbans, White Lotus Society, Righteous Fists (Boxers) and Rebęls of Heavenly Peace (Taipings).

Dynastic power was administered by educated country squires, called "Mandarins" by the Portuguese. These civil servants were chosen by imperial exams which were in theory open to all. But tests stressing memorization of complicated Chinese language and literature penalized poor people who could not take decades of study to prepare.

The Chinese did not ask the Westerners to China but they came anyway. By the 1750s, the Chinese government felt it necessary to impose severe restrictions on Western traders and diplomats. In Canton (Guangzhou) foreigners had to live on Shamian Island, could stay only six months per year, and could not bring their families. Western diplomats at the court of Peking were expected to perform the kowtow to the emperor. After being commanded to "advance, kneel, and knock head," the emissary was expected to strike his forehead on the floor with sufficient force to be heard at a distance. Protocol required nine knocks. Western diplomats were reluctant to perform this procedure. The resulting controversy impeded diplomacy for many years.

Westerners bought large quantities of Chinese tea and silk but had little to sell that Chinese wanted to buy. In the 1770s Britain began to market opium as a way to balance British purchases of Chinese goods. By 1839 opium use was so destructive to Chinese society that the emperor sent Lin Zexu to stamp it out. He surrounded the British at Canton and confiscated twenty thousand casks of opium which he publicly burned. This led to two Opium Wars which gave the British

Hong Kong, trading ports, low tariffs, and immunity to Chinese laws. Under a "most favored nation" clause (the first use of this term), a Chinese grant to one Western country was a concession to all.

Soon the West and Japan brought overwhelming industrial and military power to bear and carved up China into many spheres of influence. Western weapons wounded China's warriors, European entrepreneurs consumed her economy and Christian missionaries mocked her values. In retaliation for Manchu torture deaths of eighteen diplomats, a British army, John Bull in a China shop, demolished and looted Peking.

End of Imperial Period

As the Manchu Dynasty slowly crumbled through the waning years of the nineteenth century the Dowager Empress, Tzu-hsi's foot-long fingernails foretold the fate of the Gentry State. Dust storms, blowing in from the Gobi, powdered the Purple Forbidden Palace with layers of loess. Old photos in sepia tint capture the grainy gloom of the imperial courtyards. There in the violet dusk of empire, jaded old men, defecating in drainage ditches, ponder the golden past.

Nationalist Period

In the dying days of the Manchu Dynasty, Sun Yat-sen developed a political system based on Three People's Principles: Nationalism (opposition to both Manchu and Western imperialism), Livelihood (economic reform with land redistribution), and Democracy (after a very long period of tutelage for the masses). Sun patterned these after Lincoln's concept of government for, of, and by the people.

After a successful revolt against the Manchus in 1911, Sun was elected provisional president of a Chinese Nationalist Republic which actually controlled only a small area around Canton in southern China. The north fell under the influence of regional warlords. Sun died in 1925 and was replaced by a young military officer, Chiang Kai-shek, who had achieved prominence as commandant of the Nationalist military academy at Whompoa, near Canton.

The Chinese Communist Party, founded in 1921, was driven underground after several urban uprisings. Its leader, Mao Zedong, departed from the Marxist dogma of revolution of the urban proletariat by organizing poor peasants. For this heresy Mao was temporarily thrown out of the Chinese Communist Party. Civil War between the Nationalists and Communists continued even through the Japanese occupation in World War II. Finally, in 1949, a Nationalist government weakened by war, corruption, drought, and inflation, fled to Taiwan, leaving China to the Communists. As Mao had often said, "Political power grows from the barrel of a gun."

Communist Period

The Communist revolution of 1949 mimicked previous dynasties in many respects. Marxist teachings replaced Confucian principles as instruments to suppress individualism. Party cadres controlled the daily lives of people in much the same way as the lower gentry of the dynasties. Neither bureaucracy produced equality but the Communists preached it. No opposition was considered loyal. Opponents in both the dynastic and communist systems were treated as disloyal sons. Mao Zedong and (later) Deng Hsiao-ping were treated as emperors. The big family (the state) replaced the little family of tradition.

The structure of the Communist Party is based on democratic centralism, in which each unit elects representatives to a higher unit, ending with a central committee of roughly three hundred members, which elects a politburo of twenty, which chooses a standing committee of five or six. In practice the top leaders usually determine the promotions.

The Constitution makes the National People's Congress the highest government authority. Members are elected by local and county people's congresses. Since the Communist Party selects the candidates it has full control of government, including the civil bureaucracy, courts, and army. Mao held the top party post but never bothered to obtain a position in government.

The idea of the Chinese Communist Party as a monolith is a myth. As in most single-party systems, there are many factions. The throes of change will produce many more. These produced conflicting campaigns: the Great Leap Forward; the Hundred Flowers; invasions of Korea, Tibet, India, and Vietnam; the Cultural Revolution; trials of the Gang of Four; the Nixon Opening; and the slaughter in Tiananmen Square. The common people resigned to this panorama of political spasms call it "the changing sky."

Recent Politics

The current controversy between China's reformers and conservatives is not over replacing a command economy with a market economy but over how quickly this should be done. There are many reasons for China's opening to modern realities: the death of Mao; the need to use the United States to balance Russian power; the success of Chinese economies in Hong Kong, Singapore, and Taiwan; and the collapse of communism in Eastern Europe and the former Soviet Union. The leaders of the Chinese Communist Party realized they could only maintain power by satisfying consumer demands and encouraging foreign investment. Much of this is coming from Chinese Hong Kong, Taiwan, and Singapore. With monetary investment comes considerable Chinese cultural identity to replace that lost in Communist social pograms.

With the Nixon visit to China and the negotiations with Great Britain over Hong Kong, China assumed a prominent role in world affairs.

National Law and Local Leavening

Chinese leaders are culturally correct in saying that China should not be held to the same standards on human rights as Western nations. Western concepts of law were shaped by centuries of social compacts and revolutions from the Magna Carta through the Renaissance to the French and American Revolutions. While the Chinese saw only order in nature, the Westerners saw natural rights grounded in natural law. These "inalienable" rights were guaranteed by social contracts called constitutions.

Asians usually point to their constitutions to prove they live in democracies. But the Chinese constitution, reflecting a culture which experienced none of the above revolutions, places the group (nation) above the individual. It guarantees a daily nap but not popular elections or peaceful changes of power between competing political parties.

In China rights are really privileges derived from government. It is lawful for the state to arbitrarily define and change the role of the individual. Expressions of individuality (such as Western-style freedom of speech, press, religion) are often viewed as obstacles to stability and detriments to the national welfare.

The traditional Chinese criminal justice system has been described as one with more confessions than crimes. But a new legal code is attempting to replace rule of men with rule of law. Perhaps powerful politicians will stop intervening in due process. If so, some of the color will go out of crime; imaginative authorities in Shanghai recently punished traffic violators by making them direct traffic for a month.

The justice system with the help of local committees is very effective in preventing serious crime. Assaults are very rare and never repeated by the same criminal because assaulters are publicly executed with a single bullet in the back of the head. Yet petty theft is prevalent, as evidenced by sharp broken glass cemented into tops of walls and bars on windows.

Ever since their agonizing experience with legalism in the ancient Chin Dynasty the Chinese populace has preferred controls based on cultural traditions and human relationships rather than laws. They suspect distant governments. How can they understand local situations? Chinese want local leavening of laws through resolutions of problems by people who know them best: family, villagers, neighbors. Realists to the core, they feel committed to other people rather than abstract legislative concepts. A resident committee in each locality is charged with implementing laws. It does this in a traditional way by balancing the interests of all concerned. The committee is chosen from volunteers, mostly retired people or active housewives, who bring public respect to the job. The committee serves local government by mediating disputes, watching the movements of residents and visitors, scheduling health clinics, judging petty crimes and managing the census, family planning, and sanitation. Settlement of auto accidents might be added to this caseload.

Ethnic and Clan Conflict

The loosening of central power in China as in Eastern Europe has permitted the return of old ethnic and clan rivalries. Two recent incidents serve as examples.

In the "7 October Incident" of 1993, Chinese paramilitary troops stormed a mosque to control an uprising of Hui Moslems in the Qinghai provincial capital of Xining. Tens of thousands of rioters attacked police stations, hijacked planes, and blocked traffic. The cause of this disturbance was publication of a book portraying a Moslem praying next to a pig, a religious insult. The Hui population, numbering about nine million, is large enough to cause considerable trouble. China has many such ethnic minorities.

In Hunan Province a thousand year old clan system, dormant in the Mao era, is reviving. As the central government returns land to families and villages, clan leaders are asserting power. Women are being relegated to feudal status by denial of their inheritance rights and choices in marriage. Competition between clans has led to armed clashes. According to the *China Legal Daily* over five hundred people have been killed in clan violence in Hunan Province in the past few years. The clan battle of Matianxu in September 1993, lasted three days and left dozens of dead and injured. There is considerable potential for clan conflict because China has many clans in many provinces.

Political Prospects

Like most of the rest of the world China's foreign and domestic politics are being driven by economics rather than ideology.

In ways the situation in China is similar to that of the 1930s, except today economic czars in the south pull power from the northern capital. In the past northern warlords operated independently of a southern capital. The powerful adrenaline of a booming economy in southern China will stimulate great changes in the Communist Party, state bureaucracy, army, and emerging business class. China is compressing hundreds of years of Western change into a few decades as one-fourth of mankind is raised from poverty. The pace may be too fast to avoid political upheavals. There could be repeats of the June 1989 massacre in Tiananmen Square.

Taiwan and Singapore have proven that multi-party government is not needed for successful Chinese capitalism. Yet some political reforms are sorely needed: elimination of economic fiefdoms, reduction of arbitrary decisions, more transparent economic policies, and better tolerance of criticism designed to uncover mistakes. Corruption sometimes reaches Italian intensity. The government is addressing some of these problems.

Hong Kong

Soon after Captain Charles Elliot acquired Hong Kong he received an angry letter from the British foreign secretary, Lord Palmerston, chastising him for adding "a barren island with hardly a house on it" to the British Empire. Queen Victoria's husband, Albert, was so amused at the addition he turned it into a family joke.

As Hong Kong grew in wealth things became serious. The colony became valuable to its neighbors. When the Communists came to power in China in 1949, they could have grabbed Hong Kong in less time than it takes to fry rice. But they did not. In 1967 riots rocked the colony. A Red militia invaded Hong Kong, killing police. Panic spread, property prices plummeted, and the governor kept a plane ready at Kai Tak Airport for a quick exit. But Beijing halted the disruption. Even in the throes of the Cultural Revolution, the Chinese government recognized a takeover of Hong Kong would result in lost foreign exchange and property losses for the many banks, hotels, and office buildings it owned in the colony.

Today most of economic Hong Kong is located in mainland China. From boats in the Pearl River or speeding trains one sees a continuous strip of factories and commercial buildings stretching from Hong Kong to Canton (Guangzhou). Hong Kong telephone and electric companies serve the mainland. The Hong Kong-based airline, Cathay Pacific, keeps its maintenance and repair facilities on the mainland. At least a fifth of Hong Kong's currency circulates in Guangdong Province. Indeed, many of the cities I visited there refused to take money issued by the Chinese government. Only Hong Kong dollars were accepted in hotels and restaurants.

The economies of southern China, Hong Kong, and Taiwan are so intertwined that a tragedy for one would hurt all. Barring an importune uprising in Hong Kong the Chinese government will benefit by allowing Hong Kong to prosper. China wants to woo Taiwan back to the bosom of mother

China. A draconian policy toward Hong Kong would preclude this. Under China, Hong Kong will be capitalist but not very democratic, as it was under the British. But it will no longer be a colony. Instead it will be the capital of southern China.

PART TWO

Economy and Business

China has one of the fastest growing economies in the world. As home of a quarter of the human race and a substantial portion of its resources, it has great potential. Economic and business events are moving so rapidly that the elderly policy wonks in Beijing sometimes have difficulty keeping up. The booming Chinese business arena offers both rewards and risks. While the dangers are not as obvious as the typhoons, shipwrecks, scurvy, pirates, malaria, and cholera faced by early American traders, they are nevertheless real.

To operate successfully in China you will need to know how its economy developed, how it functions, and its strengths and weaknesses. This section will also help you with some of the practical problems of doing business. These topics include information on how to get help in doing business in China, standards of commercial etiquette, and techniques for business negotiation.

The business and economic environment in China is based on the cultural and social foundations just covered. These are the primary determinants of business behavior.

4. A Brief Economic History

The Dynastic Economy

Some twenty thousand years ago a fertile area in Central Asia dried up and became the Gobi Desert. Its inhabitants moved into what is now northwest China and became early Chinese. Their economy, like those in Egypt, Mesopotamia, and the Indus, was established on the flood plain of a great river, the Yellow, which provided silt and water for agriculture. The ability to store surplus food freed time for a variety of industries. By 2000 B.C. the Chinese produced sophisticated pottery. This was followed by bronze (1400 B.C.) and iron (700 B.C.) metallurgy. By 200 A.D. steel was produced using piston bellows. Many of these achievements were well ahead of similar European developments.

In the dynastic system the governing gentry, peasants, craftsmen, and merchants had distinct roles to play. Government control of the economy was tight. It managed storage and distribution facilities and maintained monopolies, at various times, of metals, silk, tea, and salt (essential for people on grain diets). Even labor was monopolized. The corvée system required peasants to work a month a year for the government, usually on dike construction and repair.

The peasants, with status ranking them just under government officials, were the heart of the dynastic economy. Chinese agriculture was based on labor-intensive gardening rather than extensive farming as we know it. Arable land was always small relative to population. Most forests were destroyed early in China's history. Scarcity of oil and fuel led to invention of the wok, which could stir-fry quickly using little oil and straw for the fire.

When a peasant farmer died his land was split equally among all his sons. Plots thus became smaller and smaller. In spite of rigorous use of labor, water, human and animal fertilizer, and multi-cropping (two or three per year), many plots could not support a family. If some members obtained government or craft employment the family could survive. Otherwise it starved.

The merchant was at the bottom of society under officials, peasants, and craftsmen. Only soldiers, who had no status, were lower than the merchant. Neither shopkeeper nor trader manufactured anything. They preferred shortages to increase prices. A Mandarin term for one ignobly engaged in shuffling goods around for a profit is *mai mai ren*, "buy-sell person." At various times merchants were forbidden ownership of land, houses, and silk and had to wear shoes with clashing colors to denote low status. Taxes were heavy.

China was so vast, its resources so ample, its economy so self-sufficient that most trade was internal. The Grand Canal, linking numerous rivers with the coast, provided transport for such commodities as rice, cotton, iron, tea, salt, silk, timber and horses.

Traders not tied to specific locations did better. For one out at sea or deep in the desert the emperor and his tax collectors were at the best distance for business. By the tenth century Chinese junks, often in violation of law, were plying the waters of the South China Sea establishing independent communities in Southeast Asia. Enterprises such as trade on the Silk Road which wound its way for four thousand miles to Tyre, Lebanon, produced fortunes by providing silk for the togas of Roman caesars. Some of the profits were used to suborn officials.

Most of China's international trade began on the southern coast because it was nearest sea routes to Malacca, India, and Europe. Also southern rivers, unlike those in the north, were free of ice and navigable year round. China's southern coastal provinces soon became more cosmopolitan than the rest of the country. They acted as windows to the world, centers for foreign trade, and departure points for emigrants. Even today most Chinese-Americans trace ancestry to southern China.

For a long time China's landed officials placed many impediments in the way of industry and foreign trade. They wanted no competition for the agricultural system they controlled. High interest, short-term loans flowed to desperate peasants. Low interest, long-term money was not available to develop industries. Chinese enterprises made money, not by producing more goods, but by obtaining a government monopoly, raising prices, and squeezing the market.

In spite of this, some large-scale industries, such as silk and cotton textiles and ceramics developed by 1500 A.D., the middle of the Ming Dynasty.

When the Manchus (Qing Dynasty) conquered China in 1644, these nomadic horsemen reduced the size of industry, increased manufacturing taxes and closed the door on foreign trade. The only port allowed to stay open was Canton; its trade was limited to Southeast Asia. China's trading door remained closed until forced open by Western soldiers and warships in the nineteenth century. By then the Manchus, lost in corruption and debauchery, helpless in the face of floods and famines, had lost the mandate of heaven. The West arrived during the final years of a dying dynasty.

Opening of China

The opening of China began with the closing of the Silk Road in the eighth century by Arab armies invigorated by the new religion of Islam. This forced trade by sea. Ironically, the first vessels in this trade to show up in the harbors of southern China were Arab dhows. From the very start the opening of China was a commercial activity. American traders, somewhat late to arrive, competed with the Portuguese, Dutch, Spanish, and British by purchasing tea, camphor, silks and spices and selling the only import China wanted: kerosene, "oil for the lamps of China."

Foreign traders residing in China were factors, balancing inventory, accounts receivable and loans, so their warehouses, offices and living quarters were known as factories. These lined the banks of the Pearl River in Canton.

The Chinese government confined Western influence by building high walls around the factories allowing access only from the river. Western traders were not allowed out of their designated compounds but could visit the Portuguese enclave at Macau. No Westerner could bring his family to China.

At one time foreign traders were restricted to Whompoa, a port about a dozen miles down the Pearl River from Canton. Here white-winged sailing ships arrived to anchor in a forest of masts. Shore leave for Western seamen was restricted to dingy docks which were crammed with bars and bordellos, smoking food stands, and casinos on carts. Life, like commerce, was a gamble.

Those who broke the rule separating Chinese and Westerners were dealt with rather harshly. One Paou-pang started China's tourist industry by illegally organizing trips through the scenic countryside for Westerners. His sentence was death by a thousand cuts. This traditional means of execution was performed by four specialists with tiny but very sharp knives who cut off slices of flesh beginning with the finger and toes. On the way to Paou-pang's torso they prolonged the execution by taking care not to puncture arteries. About the same time the government burned Paou-pang's village, beheaded his entire family, and destroyed everything within twenty miles of the incident. This was serious: No tourists! It was not an auspicious beginning for the China travel industry.

Crisis of 1839 and Opium Wars

Soon Westerners began to wonder why they should put up with all these restrictions, particularly when the West had more and better weapons. The opium wars ostensibly began over a brawl between a drunk British sailor and a sober Chinese. In reality it involved the need to push opium on the Chinese because there were few other Western products the Chinese wanted to buy. After the Chinese Commissioner Lin destroyed a store of British opium, war erupted. After two opium wars and several treaties China paid for the destroyed opium, ceded Hong Kong to Britain, opened additional ports, and granted Westerners immunity to Chinese law. At the request of the American Commodore Kearny, a "most favored nation" clause was added, making a Chinese grant to one Western country a gift to all. Though the Chinese officials considered Americans "second-class Englishmen," they hoped to play the English and Americans against each other.

The West had the preponderance of power due to its industrial revolution. China, unwilling to modernize even for its own self-interest, soon suffered the death of a thousand cuts. Large foreign enclaves were carved from its body. A flood of foreign imports destroyed China's emerging industries. Western technology, fired with an almost religious commercial zeal, consumed the country. With the end of slavery in the United States thousands of deceived or coerced Chinese were transported to America to fill the demand for cheap labor making the word "Shanghai" a verb as well as a noun.

Westerners looked at China's teeming masses and calculated the fortunes which could be made by selling each Chinese an additional inch of shirttail. Unfortunately many Chinese could not even afford shirts.

By the end of the nineteenth century China was a dumping ground for Western textiles, metal utensils, dyes, kerosene, and opium. After the loss of a war with Japan (1894-5) and the failure of the Boxer Rebellion (1900) the Chinese slowly began to recognize the need to modernize. This awareness produced a revolution which toppled the Manchu Dynasty in 1911. It was followed by weak rule by the Nationalist Party, uneasy political alliances, civil war, Japanese invasion, and the Communist Revolution of 1949. This constant turmoil precluded economic development.

Communist Period

After taking power the Chinese Communist Party began a program of socialist land reform and five-year industrial programs. Development of heavy industry became a major goal. In 1956 the government made itself a partner in all private businesses. A few years later it confiscated them all.

Mass movements such as the Great Leap Forward (1958) and the Cultural Revolution (1966-76) tried to transform the economy and the culture. Both failed. Backyard smelters were inefficient and Red Guards too destructive. Some business people were punished by such devices as being forced to wear paper handcuffs which, if torn, even during sleep, resulted in a bloody beating. Incentives disappeared with the abolition of private plots and free markets. By the time of Mao's death in 1976 the Chinese economy was moribund.

Hong Kong

At the time it was ceded to Britain, Hong Kong, with a population under a thousand, was of little importance to China. Due to coastal pirates China always located its seaports well inland, up rivers defended by forts. The British navy, however, had the guns to defend coastal enclaves.

The British quickly developed their colony, shooting tigers, cobras, and pythons that refused to vacate for parks and golf courses. A salt marsh was filled in, named Happy Valley, and developed as a race track. White mansions with broad verandas were built on the Peak. At twelve hundred feet they caught balmy breezes from the harbor. Hong Kong soon became a major supply, fuel, and transportation center, the only treaty port south of Shanghai which could accommodate large ocean-going ships. It rapidly took business away from upriver ports such as Whompoa and Canton.

The colony benefitted from the warfare of others. When it became obvious that the Communists would win the civil war, many Chinese industrialists fled (with their money) to

Hong Kong, starting textile and shoe industries. During the Korean and Vietnam wars Hong Kong became a center for American military procurement, supply, maintenance and repair, and troop recreation.

Hong Kong outlasted Mao, who died in 1976. But at midnight, June 30, 1997, it returns to China. According to the 1984 agreement with Britain, Hong Kong will keep its current economic and social system for fifty years. Not mentioned is the fact that Hong Kong's economic system has already taken over much of southern China.

Recent Reforms

Human events take some ironic twists. By the end of 1978, Deng Hsiaoping, firmly in power, reversed Mao's policies by instituting incentives and choices. By the late 1980s China's economy was booming to the extent that the infrastructure was straining and inflation was replacing stagnation.

There were many reasons for China's turn toward capitalism. Every revolution has its practical aftermath, a time when pragmatists take power from violent ideologues and begin to build. This shift took place in America when the conservatism of our Constitution replaced the fury of the Declaration of Independence. The shift in France took place when Napoleonic order replaced the anarchy of The Terror. As the collapse of communism in Eastern Europe and the Soviet Union unfolded, Deng and his associates realized their government could suffer the same fate. The best way to stay in power was to provide consumer goods. The best way to provide consumer goods was to provide incentives for capital and labor and create a market economy. Production shifted to consumer goods, foreign trade was encouraged, and special economic zones were opened to foreign investment. As Deng phrased it, "All Chinese will become equally wealthy, but some before others." It was rapidly becoming a capitalist country led by a communist party.

An additional irony involves the nexus of Marxist theory and the actual development of communism in China. The Chinese turned communist theory upside down. First, they rose to power through actions of poor peasants rather than the required urban proletariat. Secondly, they did not follow the "inevitable" Marxian progression of economies from feudal to capitalist to communist. China never experienced true feudalism or capitalism. But the failure of communism is now producing a consumer-oriented capitalism which has great vitality.

Lest we rejoice we should think of the economic problems we have had with Japan. Then imagine the challenge, in ten or twenty years, of the world's largest capitalist economy, with fifteen or twenty times the potential of Japan, led by the Chinese Communist Party!

5. A Look at China's Successful Economy

Greater China

Greater China consists of the southern coasts of China, Hong Kong, Taiwan, and the overseas Chinese in Southeast Asia. It is neither an official trading bloc nor a political entity. Instead Greater China is a freewheeling economy driven by a common culture and profits.

While most of the rest of the world has endured recession and weak growth Greater China has enjoyed a boom. The rise of Greater China may be the transcendent economic event of the next two decades. It is the only emerging economic superpower which has the potential to surpass Japan.

The building blocks for this successful machine have always been there, but they are now coming together. The parts are linked by shared Confucian values: savings discipline, passion for learning, family values, and group priorities. The ideological underbrush, an elaborate screen of political prattle, has been mostly cleared away.

Each unit of Greater China makes a distinct contribution. China offers huge resources in land and raw materials. Its labor not only produces at low cost but provides a large market for goods and services. The economy of one Chinese province, Guangdong, has grown in the mid-teens for over a decade. It accounts for a quarter of China's exports and its retail trade exceeds Hong Kong's. In recent years Guangdong has attracted as much foreign investment as the rest of China. The Pearl River area, which I visited, is rapidly becoming the world's largest industrial center. New factories, offices, and apartments appear almost overnight. The din of progress is deafening.

Hong Kong provides world-class servicing, marketing, trading, communication, and design expertise. A product may be patterned in Hong Kong, assembled in a Chinese plant financed by Taiwan, and shipped to Singapore for distribution. About a quarter of Hong Kong's currency is circulated in China.

Taiwan contributes capital, technology, and financial prowess. As the world's second largest holder of foreign currency reserves it can back projects to the hilt. Taiwanese investments are pouring into China too quickly to quantify. At last count roughly three thousand Taiwanese companies had invested over four billion dollars in more than five thousand factories in China. The impact of Taiwanese investment is felt as far away as China's remote Xinjiang Province.

Many overseas Chinese return to their ancestral homes with cash in their pockets. Chinese from Singapore to San Francisco are financing the real estate boom on China's gold coast.

My visit to Guangzhou confirmed the prevalence of consumer goods. Most houses and apartments flaunted television antennas tuned to Hong Kong stations transmitting commercials for items ranging from French brandy to Japanese cameras. China will never be the same!

Role of Government

What role did government play to bring this all about? First, what were the goals? China's economic liberalization began in 1979 under Deng Xsiaoping with the purpose of creating a modern, prosperous industrial economy with socialist values. Western-style democracy or civil rights do not fit in the picture since, as already described, they are very alien to five thousand years of Chinese culture.

Beijing's taste for intervention in the economy has been both sweet and sour. Some decisions have been wise. Instead of quickly selling or disbanding state industries (as in some nations in Eastern Europe), China has chosen to let the normal growth of private industry slowly replace state enterprises. This has been much less disruptive. Yet, construction policy, which favored factories for a long time, caused a severe shortage of office space. Government direction and ownership remain higher than in the West.

Western development theorists are taking another look at an entrenched wisdom which preaches a prerequisite of democracy for modern economies based on free markets. In Singapore, Taiwan, South Korea, and Thailand, heavy-handed manipulation of industry and trade by authoritarian rulers produced some of the world's fastest growing economies.

The Chinese government is employing the same tools of success used in other East Asian oligarchies: directing credit to industries which grow exports, subsidizing technology, protecting infant industries with tariffs, and encouraging only private enterprises which conform with government goals.

Special Economic Zones (SEZs)

Special Economic Zones worked well in Taiwan. They are designed to attract foreign manufacturing technology by eliminating some taxes, abating bureaucracy, and allowing factories flexibilities in wages and production. Most manufacturing in China's SEZs involves consumer electronics, watches, home appliances, and transportation equipment. Joint ownership is encouraged and some profits can be repatriated. Rules are always changing so you should write the Chinese government for the most recent regulations or hire an international attorney.

In addition to SEZs there are a variety of other special areas. Fourteen coastal cities are "open" and other areas fulfill specialized economic roles. Special zones, appealing in purpose, are sometimes appalling in practice. "Spontaneous," unofficial zones, formed for illegal activities such as smuggling, black market, and currency violations are regularly closed by the government.

Shenzhen, on Hong Kong's border, is the largest special zone. Once a sleepy fishing village, it has Hong Kong's glitter because Hong Kong Chinese are its largest investors. Zhuhai SEZ is just north of Macau, across the bay from Hong Kong. It offers a full range of modern hotel, convention, and meeting facilities. The architecture of its incredible shopping center is based on the design of Beijing's imperial palaces. Shantou, formerly Swatou, on the coast, is the second largest city in Guangdong Province. With its twin city, Chaozhou, it is often called Chaoshan. It is the home of Hakka people and their variety of tasty dipping sauces. Xiamen SEZ, the fourth, formerly Amoy, is another nugget on China's "gold coast." Here thousands of Taiwanese have invested in tourism, manufacturing, and agriculture.

Hainan, the fifth SEZ, is in a class by itself. Some time ago Beijing lent one-and-a-half billion dollars to Hainan SEZ officials to build roads, docks, utilities, and industrial parks. Instead these dignitaries bribed the Chinese navy to smuggle in 89,000 cars, 2.6 million TV sets, 122,000 motorcycles, and 252,000 VCRs, which they used the loan money to buy. These were sold at four times the purchase cost to eager Chinese buyers. Only after Beijing noticed a huge drain in Chinese foreign currency reserves did it discover the naughty behavior of the SEZ managers. By then half the billion-and-a-half dollars had disappeared into celestial bliss. Though local papers referred to the culprits as "rascals," their punishments, quite imaginative, were sufficient to "liberate their thinking." Lately a gamut of industrial projects, from textiles to communications, has been developed under the watchful eyes of federal adminstrators. Hainan is worth visiting for its white, pristine beaches, palm-shrouded hills, and ARCO pipeline.

In Suzhou, fifty miles west of Shanghai, a consortium led by the tiny nation of Singapore is setting up an industrial township. This will be a clone of Singapore itself, complete with factories, offices, shopping centers, and draconian laws imposing fines on citizens who chew gum or fail to flush the toilets.

There are three special municipalities: Tianjin, Beijing, and Shanghai. The national government is developing Shanghai as a counter to the growing power of Guangdong. New economic zones include Hongqiao Area, Minhang Economic and Technical Zone, Pudong, and Caohejing Hi-tech Park. After getting lost in the Shanghai Orient Shopping Center I thought I was in Hong Kong or Singapore.

Investment Laws

China's economy exists in a twilight zone between capitalism and socialism. Joint ventures, which China encourages through China International Trust and Investments, involve compromises between the two systems. Investment laws and regulations are arcane and enforced in desultory fashion. Consider real estate as an example. There are no national standards for real estate laws. Land can not be purchased but the right to use it can be bought with a premium payment. Taxes, bribes, and fees are arbitrary and unpredictable. Roughly a quarter of the premium plus other payments must be made before any government construction permits are approved.

Who would be willing to develop real estate on this basis? Certainly not legalistic Westerners. Fortunes are being made in the China coast real estate boom by overseas Chinese from Hong Kong, Taiwan, Singapore, and Indonesia who adhere to cultural norms and use connections. Here again the past is present.

The rewards are ample for companies willing to deal with the complexities of China's investment laws and deal through Chinese agents familiar with the culture. The roll of successful foreign firms in China reads like a Who's Who in world business: Singer Sewing, R. J. Reynolds, Johnson Wax, Lufthansa, Matsushita, Volkswagen, to mention but a few. Coke's sales in China have been estimated at more than forty per cent growth per year.

Agriculture

With less than seven per cent of the world's arable land, China must feed twenty-three per cent of the world's population. Agriculture is still the basis of the Chinese economy. China is one of the top three world producers of wheat, fish, potatoes, eggs, tea, silk, soybeans, peanuts, corn, rice, tobacco, and pork. Almost half of the pigs in the world live in China.

China's agricultural development will likely follow Taiwan's. When farmers there were allowed to choose their crops and sell them on free markets, rather than grow commodity crops for sale to the state, agriculture prospered. Agricultural entrepreneurs soon learned a lot of money could be made in value-added export crops such as canned mushrooms and oranges, exotic fruits, and pond-farmed shrimp.

Mining and Manufacturing

China's natural resources are vast. It places near the top in world production of coal, tungsten, energy, steel, chemicals, and textiles.

The economy of the Middle Kingdom is booming because it is learning to turn its natural resources into consumer goods. Demand is huge. For every thousand Chinese there are only two cars, three refrigerators, five telephones, and eight television sets. The average Chinese drinks less than a gallon of sodas per year.

Chinese have buying power since rents are low, about two dollars per month, and many work underground jobs in addition to official positions.

Trade

For five thousand years (until the late 1970s) foreign trade was never a significant part of China's economy. Though newly opened to trade, China usually has a favorable balance (which is more than you can say for the United States). Hong Kong and China are each other's largest trading partners. After 1997 this will be internal. There are ample opportunities for all. Vast amounts of Chinese capital is being funneled into purchase of foreign goods and services related to electrical power generation and transmission, port and harbor construction, and petroleum extraction and refining. China needs machine tools and technology for production of consumer goods which can be exported to pay for imports. China's exports consist primarily of commodities, low-cost labor products, and military hardware including missiles to the Mideast.

China's trading bureaucracy is being decentralized so rapidly it is confusing. The Ministry of Foreign Economic Relations and Trade supervises a variety of foreign trade corporations which are supplemented by a motley array of municipal, provincial, special zone, and private entities. All of these negotiate trade. Sometimes they compete with each other.

Finance

China saves about thirty-five per cent of its gross domestic product, roughly the same as most East Asian countries. Yet this is not nearly enough to finance its burgeoning economy. Stock markets at Shenzhen and Shanghai have to struggle to keep up with China's demand for capital. Hong Kong helps to fill this need by arranging sale of initial stock issues for Chinese companies. This function will probably accelerate after Hong Kong's return to China.

The Shanghai Stock Exchange was closed when it was liberated by the Communist Army in 1950. Its elaborate building survived to see the return of the exchange in 1986. Thinking it had to be seen to be believed, I went to see it. Chinese are impulsive gamblers and the lack of security regulations leads to wild markets reminiscent of ours before the New Deal. Prices are volatile, trading thin. There are many insiders and many companies keep three books: one for the company, one for taxes, and one for shareholders. It is permissible for a company to issue a block of stock, watch the price go up, sell its treasury shares, then issue a second block carrying warrants or other rights which destroy the value of the first block. Unlike the New York Exchange, Shanghai's lists companies with many classes of stock. Nevertheless, demand for stocks is so great that lotteries are sometimes used to decide rights to purchase. Foreigners are allowed to buy shares but there are certain restrictions.

Labor

China's labor is cheap. Workers are willing to labor long hours for little income, yet they do not seem as driven as many American workers. In Guangdong laborers with basic skills earn roughly $150 per month. This compares to roughly one thousand dollars per month in Hong Kong and two thousand dollars per month in the United States.

A Chinese work week now consists of forty-four hours. China's labor force is five times that of the United States. Its income is grossly underestimated because many workers punch in at government jobs and then leave for more lucrative positions in the underground economy.

Labor productivity is improving. In the past a worker's job was an "iron rice bowl" which could not be broken. This is no longer true.

Transportation and Communication

Chinese transportation and communications are improving rapidly because they leapfrog steps in Western development. For example, wireless cellular phone service, which is expanding rapidly, does not depend on slow tedious installation of wires. It is quicker and cheaper to lay concrete for runways than for thousands of miles of roads.

Chinese air traffic is growing about thirty per cent per year. Many new regional airlines are opening. Firms such as Boeing are benefitting from their orders.

China's navigable rivers and railway system, both over-burdened, are the mainstay of cargo transportation. The formation of new bus companies is burgeoning but this mode of transport is inhibited by a generally poor road network. The geography of China, a pastiche of isolated valleys and rugged ranges, channels rail and road routes into inefficient, round-about doglegs.

Harbors are being improved to accommodate increasing foreign trade. Shanghai is a key port because of its location near the nexus of the Grand Canal and a network of navigable rivers reaching far to the west.

After 1997 Hong Kong will continue to be the transportation and communication hub of southern China. Its new airport and port facilities are designed to handle four times current cargo traffic by 2011. Access to Guangzhou is improving with construction of a high-speed highway from Hong Kong. Chinese commerce will continue to be dependent on Hong Kong for instant world-wide transmission of financial data and transactions.

Travel and Tourism

Chinese authorities, with their love for control, still prefer group tours. The variety is increasing. Foreigners can now visit some space centers where officials pretend visitors are rocket scientists. An army division near Tianjin offers a soldier-for-a-day tour involving greeting by an honor guard and training on bayonet, personal combat, and automatic weapons courses. So far no tourist-soldiers have been killed in action.

Individual travel is now widely available but more difficult.

Hong Kong

After the integration of Hong Kong, China's economy will be third in size in the world after the United States and Japan. Hong Kong will contribute transportation, trade, finance, and communication. During the embargo of China which followed the communist takeover, Hong Kong developed light manufacturing to replace lost trade. These production enterprises, ranging from textiles to toys, long ago saturated Hong Kong's limited space and sprawled into nearby China, employing roughly four million workers. China, in return, shows its bullishness on Hong Kong by heavy real estate, banking and industrial investments. Hong Kong and southern China are already an economic unit.

The change is most striking at the border. When I first visited Lo Wu, in 1958, visitors from Hong Kong to China had to stumble over a rickety railway bridge and smile obsequiously at a grim-faced guard wearing a Mao badge. In my 1993 visit I was swept along by a fissiparous horde of harried commuters who entered China with quick flashes of identification cards. This time the guard had the servile smile.

Economic Prospects

It will be interesting to see how China's leaders after thirty years of failure in managing a centralized command economy deal with the problems of free markets.

Western economic theories may not provide the answers. These consider money to be a commodity. Increasing the supply should lower its value and interest rates. Yet increasing the supply in the United States in the late 1970s led to inflation and *higher* interest rates. Economic theory also says that adding to a national deficit increases interest rates due to crowding out of private borrowers by government needs to finance the deficit. Yet large annual increases in fiscal deficits during the Reagan years were accompanied by sharply *lower* interest rates! In Shanghai and Guangzhou I met government functionaries who were blissfully unaware of such colossal gaps between reality and theories propounded by Western advocates of the dismal science. Since economies are reactive, they are more likely to be influenced by individuals acting within cultural norms than by arcane machinations of policymakers. Western econobabble may have as little utility as the communist slogans of the past.

A few observations are indisputable. Aided by its sheer size and Confucian values, China will find its own way. Within a decade, if trends continue, China and an integrating Taiwan could together be the world's leading economy.

6. Economic and Business Problems

Overheating

China's economy is "too much of a good thing." Annual growth in the mid-teens has produced rampant inflation, excessive demand, severe shortages, and exorbitant stock and real estate speculation. In myriad villages small-time speculators meet in bamboo boiler-rooms to *chaogu*, "stir-fry" their stock portfolios over open telephone lines. It is a system of finance fraught with pyramid schemes, false letters of credit, commodity purchases with worthless IOUs, letters of credit drawn on imaginary banks, and incendiary inflation exceeding twenty per cent in some cities.

At the Celestial Happiness Stock Brokerage in Shanghai I saw ninety-day forward options sold for picked fruit, a commodity unqualified for futures contracts in the United States.

A 1993 World Bank report challenged the prevailing wisdom that decentralization of the Chinese economy is always good and centralization is always bad. It recommended stronger government macroeconomic management including reduction of import barriers, creation of labor markets rather than more commercial enterprises, construction of roads rather than more factories, and increased regulation of competition rather than prices. The report concluded that "a market economy does not necessarily require less government, just different government." The regnant question: can China's leaders, after a forty-year reign of error in which they made a mess of a command economy, now fine-tune a free one?

In cooling the economy the government sometimes acts like a draconian dragon. Thousands of economic development zones, which diverted money to dubious schemes, have been closed. Some bold moguls, offering versions of silver bullets (bribes) have been jailed. Some construction of luxury housing, hotels, and golf courses has been canceled. Some raw-land speculators have been forced to build low-income housing. In every case the offers could not be refused.

Protectionism

In 1983 China retaliated for American textile quotas by halting purchases of soybeans, cotton, and synthetic fibers. Many trade conflicts similar to this example were quickly understood by both parties and resolved. Other impediments to trade which involve human rights and arms exports seem to be beyond the cultural ken of both sides.

As explained in previous chapters East Asian cultures value the group over individuals. Torture of political dissidents is as Chinese as fried rice. Callow complaints will not alter this five thousand year old fact. American protectionism based on divergent cultural values could result in thousands of Boeing workers losing their jobs because Beijing police beat up a lone demonstrator. One of every six Boeing planes is sold to China.

In the same way the United States, one of the largest exporters of military hardware, takes a curiously moralistic approach to foreign sales of Chinese military technology. In August 1993, after months of indecision, the Clinton administration, responding to Chinese arms exports, halted some sales of American satellites to China. China, dependent on arms sales for hard cash to modernize its military, stopped purchasing some American consumer goods. At this point Washington hinted it might deny China most-favored-nation-status.

Americans opposed to China's family planning and abortion clinics pressured Congress to pass a resolution asking the Olympic Committee to reject China's bid to host the Olympics in 2000, which it did.

Chinese and American policies which jumble free trade, military balances, and self-righteous arrogance could cause considerable economic mischief, such as a worldwide trade war.

Bureaucracy

According to Franz Kafka every revolution leaves behind a scum of bureaucracy. China's is no different. All institutions fall behind the pace of change because of conservative hierarchies. Instead of seeking creative solutions to the problems of progress, they focus on compulsive collection and compilation of precise trivia, a form of bureaucratic masturbation which produces no babies.

Parties in power for long periods become deeply corrupt. Here again China is no different. Much of its bureaucracy is based on avarice pressure-cooked in an overheated economy.

There are no free egg rolls. Payoffs are part of the system. They have long been an essential form of proper etiquette. In China what we call bribery only becomes a problem when its leaps the limits of the cultural norm. Perhaps that is happening now. Guangdong has to pay higher taxes for more autonomy. Government functionaries funnel such funds into special projects. Much of the rest is used to subsidize money-losing state enterprises.

Sometimes the perquisites of public office extend across borders. Cadres and military officials in Guangdong order cars by make, year, and optional equipment. Within a few days underlings will steal the cars in Hong Kong and deliver them to their bosses.

Greed

Capitalism thrives on self-interest but too much greed destroys it. Inflation, shortages, and wide differences in income created by excessive avarice brought the Communists to power. Traditional Chinese business was based on cornering the market and squeezing the customer.

Many Western firms have seen their Chinese fortune cookies crumble. Remy Martin was ready to make wine in Tianjin when it learned its "joint venture" partner was already producing wine for sale from partnership grapes. Because Cantonese oranges were priced like champagne, a Beatrice Foods orange juice project failed to make a red cent. Thousands of mediocre $250 per night hotel rooms remained vacant until anxious managers realized the travel industry was a world market.

Rich Coasts, Poor Interior

How are you going to keep them down on the farm when the coasts have Levi's, Cokes, and Madonna videos? Compared to the frenetic commotion and flamboyant color of China's coasts, the interior areas are dark and doleful. Peasants crucified with cans of liquified human feces hanging from wooden shoulder yokes fertilize the fields. Coastal speculators feed fears of famine by buying future crops. Selling of children, a practice not seen since the 1930s, is on the rise. Many interior areas are off-limits to Westerners.

The Chinese press estimates as many as fifty million rural Chinese, tired of incomes averaging fifty dollars a year, have washed their hands of the fields and left for the neon-lit life of the coastal cities. Here high walls, such as Shenzhen's, and required work skills block employment. I had difficulty getting to the ticket booth at the train station in Guangzhou because it serves as a haven for countless homeless drifters. Some join crime gangs while others fall prey to "snake heads" who hiss promises of fortunes awaiting in America. Many end up working for nothing in Chinese restaurants and laundries in the United States in order to compensate Chinese crime syndicates for their ocean trips.

Inland governors gripe: "While coastal areas are being energetically developed, what should the inland provinces do?" "If policies favor only coastal exports how will the interior modernize?"

Before we place blame we should consider the human costs of our own industrial revolution. At what price progress?

Military Conflicts?

Any military hostility in Asia affects China and its economy. In preparation China has increased its military spending by annual double digits for decades. At a time the United States is reducing its armed forces China's military establishment is improving its capabilities for massive airlifting, night fighting, vertical (helicopter borne) envelopment, ground-air tactics, electronic countermeasures, and tactical nuclear weaponry. Future adversaries may learn a lesson. When you play musical chairs with elephants the chairs tend to break.

There are many Asian powder kegs waiting for a match: the Spratley Island oil dispute, a paranoid nuclear North Korea, and conflicts over the rights of sea passage in the straits off Singapore. Most have economic causes and all have economic ramifications.

China is not the only Asian nation preparing for armed conflict. India and Pakistan have formidable military structures. Japan, now spending thirty-five billion dollars a year on its self-defense forces, has the third largest military organization in the world. Indonesia purchased the entire navy of the former East Germany. Vietnam still has the second largest army in the region.

Population and Pollution

China, similar to most newly industrializing nations, is more concerned with providing employment for its mushrooming population than restraining pollution. Due to a baby boom during the Cultural Revolution over ten million new workers enter the job market each year. Private enterprise, now half the economy, must expand to provide employment.

In many industrial areas air and water pollution are appalling. Chinese, heady with the first fruits of a modern economy, ignore these blemishes. In Shanghai an open industrial sewer is called the River of Love, a name similar to America's Love Canal. On a train leaving the station I wondered why everyone had a cup with a lid, until I noticed mine was filled with soot and coal ashes from the locomotive. An old Chinese man, a wizened wisp, kept pointing to my cup, repeating "Mu tan cha." So that was what I was drinking, "char tea"!

Integration of Hong Kong

Business dislikes uncertainty. After the massacre in Tiananmen Square many Hong Kong merchants and manufacturers left the colony. They were joined by former refugees from China to Hong Kong who fear the 1997 takeover. They went to Seattle and Vancouver to build office towers and condominiums. Hong Kong Bank has moved its headquarters to London, Jardines to Bermuda. Over fifty thousand Hong Kong residents, mostly professionals and managers, have left Hong Kong each year since the massacre. Singapore places ads in Hong Kong papers promising immediate citizenship to Hong Kong residents with certain skills.

As 1997 approaches Hong Kong whistles in the dark. If it sticks to business rather than politics there should be no problems. If it controls its dissent there should be no problems. Under the British there were no real opposition parties and little democracy. The former colony might not find it difficult to get used to Chinese rule.

A stable and prosperous Hong Kong is essential to China's economic growth. Where else can deficit-ridden Chinese state enterprises travel the capitalist road by raising millions of dollars through issuance of initial public stock offering?

Problem Avoidance

Avoidance of problems is itself a problem. Because the government of China, like all Chinese, wants to "save face," negative information which would be common knowledge in the West is classified secret. This includes news regarding traffic fatalities, suicide rates, crime statistics, and effects of natural disasters. Aircraft accidents are rarely reported unless foreigners are killed or injured. Until this Chernobyl attitude is dissipated, pressing problems will remain unsolved.

In a similar fashion the government penchant for secret decision-making is not conducive to business investment. Recently the government announced a goal of "transparent" decision-making so business can anticipate clear and constant policies.

7. *Doing Business with the Chinese*

Opportunities and Risks

Opportunities for Western business abound in China's Four Modernizations: agriculture, industry, national defense, and science and technology. Though China has a wealth of natural resources, shortages of raw materials are chronic. This augurs well for companies involved in mineral extraction. Mid-tech companies such as those involved in production of motor vehicles, oil refineries, and power generation and transmission will benefit by China's exploding economy.

Companies looking for business opportunities should realize that China is skipping some traditional phases of economic development. Particularly in infrastructure China is going right to the top: cellular and satellite communication rather than wire, new airports more than new roads. One must always ask: "What makes China different?"

It is not easy to scale the Chinese wall. Today's transformation of China's economy is far more revolutionary than anything that happened in the Communist era.

During my 1993 visit to China I conducted an informal survey of Western executives to identify the most common risks. Mentioned most was China's preposterous pricing mechanism. This is a vestige of the traditional practice of cornering a market and milking it for all it can bear. If your Chinese business partner tries this kind of "squeeze," your company will be caught in the web of international price competition and left in a cocoon of spider fiber twisting in the wind. Other risks identified included poor quality control, excessive valuations of Chinese contributions to joint ventures, inadequate utilities and transportation, and arbitrary application of investment and trade laws by avaricious officials. Several Western executives told me their Chinese counterparts recognized these problems but proferred patience: "We are working on it."

Establishing a Business

Before you establish a business in China you will want to become familiar with applicable investment laws. The Chinese government offers many incentives for investors. Though codified, they are constantly changing and vary in application according to the whims of specific Chinese negotiating teams. The information here can be used as a general guide but there is no substitute for competent legal or professional advice capable of investigating greater detail and recent changes. Incentives might include tax reductions and holidays, partial or complete waivers.of export and import fees, cheap land rents, sales rights within China, and repatriation of after-tax profits. A lot depends on how much the Chinese side wants your project and how hard you bargain.

Chinese labor laws also bear investigation. The All-China Federation of Trade Unions now requires foreign-funded firms to set up trade unions. This decision came on the heels of a notorious incident in which managers of a Japanese-operated hotel in Shanghai strip-searched two waitresses accused of theft, thus evoking painful memories of World War II Japanese occupation.

Joint ventures are the most common arrangements though others, such as licensing, are available. A Chinese trade manager told me, "Joint ventures can be arranged quite quickly, in only two or three years." So do not expect a quick kill. It is better in most industries to start slowly at low cost. Develop a profitable small business before expanding.

There are several types of joint ventures. In equity joint ventures both sides contribute money. Contractual joint ventures involve land, labor, machinery, or raw materials.

Joint ventures create their own opportunities and risks. They provide partners who know the culture and local business scene. But you might find yourself in a higher, broader, and deeper commitment than you expected. Your partner, thinking in Chinese time-frames, might require your participation until the venture is fully formed, perhaps a few hundred years.

In a joint venture *guanxi*, connections of mutual favoritism, can be as important as contracts. Overseas Chinese establish *guanxi* with influential mainlanders through carefully selected gifts and favors and shared experiences. Chinese feel secure with the informal uncertainties of *guanxi* arrangements while Westerners sometimes suffer intolerable anxieties over airtight clauses of signed contracts.

Chinese Business Organization and Operation

China's business reflects its unique culture and history. These emphasize group values, conformity, and connections. To understand how Chinese businesses organize and operate, we need to look at each functional area: management, human resources, accounting, finance, marketing, and advertising.

Though Chinese managers possess considerable decision-making power, they also are influenced by a tradition of group importance. A Chinese business leader is not likely to consider a decision until every subordinate has indicated approval by stamping an imprint on the proposal with a personal chop. These chops, stamps of wood or stone rather than rubber, leave records indicating responsibility for decisions. Since managers at all levels can suffer for stamping chop approvals on the wrong proposals, decisions tend to be delayed, sometimes long enough for the problem to go away. If the entire group should agree, accountability will rest with the *dan-wei* (work unit), not individuals. Ideally everyone will be responsible and no one.

If you plan, as a Westerner, to insert yourself into a Chinese business, perhaps a joint venture as a manager, you will need to recognize that management is culturally specific. Chinese businesses mirror the values of Chinese culture. Failure to understand the culture will lead to failure to manage.

How can you coordinate people without a deep understanding of their values and habits? Take a simple memo concerning a policy change as an example. Will it recognize cultural patterns regarding relationships between superiors and subordinates? What are the customs concerning routing and delivery of written messages? Will the form and content be appropriate to the recipient's status? What are the cultural connotations of words used?

In situations where the culture decrees the superior has all the power and the subordinate has none, the Western practice of management by mutually agreed objectives (MBOs) becomes absurd.

To effectively deploy human resources in a Chinese business one needs to understand the impact of culture on organizational behavior. In China's group-oriented society the relationship between employer and employee involves a moral component based on the mutual obligations of Confucian tradition. The employer or manager, a father figure, must protect and provide for the employee in a way the West considers paternalistic. In return the worker must show the loyalty of a son or daughter. This relationship is magnified by the fact that family or clan connections are usually more important than competence.

The sight of a Chinese employee napping on a desk evokes subtle cultural considerations. Though Chinese are willing to work long hours, many will not be rushed. This tendency is supported by the lack of incentives during the Mao era and the Constitution's guarantee of a noon nap. The government has tried to increase labor productivity by reducing lunch periods from two hours to one and posting signs saying, "Time is money." But most Chinese still take two.

Too much of a firm's creativity is in the accounting department. Many Chinese companies keep three books: one each for managers, owners, and tax collectors. In the absence of government accounting standards, imaginations run wild. Accounts receivable may be treated as cash already received. Expenses such as payoffs to officials or key customers seldom appear on income statements. Some assets are kept off the balance sheet to keep them from harm. One of a firm's most important assets, its arcane connections, is never quantified. Such practices can lead Western accountants to nervous breakdowns.

In 1994 a new law to improve accounting took effect. It requires that CPA status be earned by exams given by the Chinese Institute of Certified Public Accountants. Many procedures are standardized.

In the past Chinese companies were financed by capital assigned by the government. The trend now is for private development of capital. This is done through direct foreign investment or stock offerings. The Hong Kong exchange has been the main source of private capital but the Shanghai and Shenzhen exchanges are growing in importance. They issue special classes of shares for foreigners. China recently enhanced its ability to attract international capital by adopting market rates for foreign exchange. There should be tremendous opportunities in China for foreign firms in electronic securities trading and derivative securities such as options.

The Chinese firm is also undergoing revolutionary changes in marketing and advertising. In the past Chinese businesses, state-owned, were assigned quotas to produce products allocated to other state entities. No need to sell, make a profit, or maintain quality control. Today, with the need to market products, advertising has really opened up. Ads are everywhere: in store window displays, phone books, newspapers and magazines; on billboards, television, and radio. A television war featured Proctor and Gamble versus Unilever. Chinese journalists consider corporate news conferences a form of advertising, so they demand payoffs to attend. All this marketing and advertising is producing brand-conscious consumers. At a time when much of the West buys cheaper generics, Chinese, bored by decades of shabby Communist goods, look for labels. Some are so enthralled by big brands they keep labels, tags, and price slips on purchases even as they wear and use them.

The future of Chinese firms should be fascinating. How will they apply such Western concepts as cutthroat competition, headhunting, hostile takeovers, and making a killing? How will the Chinese business lexicon deal with golden parachutes, wolf packs, white knights, and poison pills? Will it call mass layoffs "the death of a thousand cuts?"

Guangzhou Trade Fair

The Guangzhou (Canton) Trade Fair is a major Chinese business event. It is held twice a year, from mid-April to early May, and from mid-October to early November. Invitations can be garnered from the Ministry of Foreign Economic Relations and Trade (MOFERT), its foreign trade corporations, and special zone administrations.

Hong Kong

After 1997 doing business in China will still involve Hong Kong. The former colony will remain Southeast Asia's leading financial center, a free market with no black market, no exchange controls and full acceptance of credit cards.

Free trade zones, such as Hong Kong, Aden, Panama, and the Canary Islands perform unique roles. They do not merely provide duty-free bargains for devoted shoppers. They also function as test markets for new products which must endure sharp price and quality competition in order to survive. Wealthy shoppers, unable to buy such products in protected home markets, visit these free trade zones on shopping sprees. When they return home with these products, trends and demands are set which lower trade barriers. Many world-class products rose from small debuts on the shelves of small shops in free trade zones such as Hong Kong.

It is ironic that American business people, who constantly complain about the lack of "level playing fields," often fail to use the open arenas of free trade zones to export. Instead they use these zones to buy. Selling is left to the Japanese and others. No wonder the United States has trade deficits, Japan, surpluses.

Business negotiations in Hong Kong are cutthroat. An American engineering executive I met at the Peninsula Hotel in Hong Kong told me he was staying at this opulent palace only because a "friend" had arranged to move his belongings from a cheaper hotel where he had been staying. A "friend" was also paying his bill at the Peninsula, the costs of his new tailored suits, and meals at expensive restaurants. No one in Hong Kong would accept this American's money since a "friend" had already paid the bill. Not until this American sat at the table of his first Hong Kong bargaining session did he meet his "friend," the chief negotiator for the other side!

Hong Kong's boom is an euphoriant which masks risks. Disparities between the Chinese and Hong Kong political systems are sure to produce crises. American restrictions of trade with China over issues like human rights and arms sales are likely to hurt Hong Kong. In a worst-case scenario a trade war provoked by American efforts to impose Western political values on China's five thousand year old authoritarian tradition could cause panic and collapse of the Hong Kong stock market, exchange controls, and freezing of Western assets. Without confidence Hong Kong's financial services industry would be forced to relocate, leaving empty steel and glass buildings resembling the discarded shells of sea creatures.

8. Bargaining

Making Contacts

The bargaining process begins when you start to explore business opportunities in China. As soon as you present your firm to Chinese officials, entrepreneurs, and potential partners, you will open negotiations. Your goal will be to obtain invitations to China, appointments, introductions, and information in return for potential advantages for the Chinese. Your application for government approval of your project should be the end of negotiations, not the beginning.

There are many ways to make initial contacts: The Ministry of Foreign Relations and Trade (MOFERT), its foreign trading corporations, trade fairs, technical seminars; federal, state, and local trade missions, Chinese diplomatic posts in the United States, American diplomatic posts in China, agencies such as the Department of Commerce, domestic and foreign trading companies, international business attorneys, and Hong Kong enterprises. Chapters in this book on getting help and key addresses should assist you in these efforts.

You might start with a letter of inquiry. Keep your proposal short, simple, and hypothetical. Stress the potential benefits for the Chinese. When possible mention mutual friends or contacts as possible intermediaries. Ask for an invitation to China. Without one your team will not be granted business visas. A cover letter in Mandarin will help your fledgling proposal wing its way to the appropriate bureaucratic pigeonhole.

With Whom Will You Deal?

It is important to identify key Chinese agencies and individuals as soon as possible. Through these decision-makers try to obtain an informal and hypothetical evaluation of the chances for approval and requirements for success for your project. This will not be easy. In recent years negotiating authority, once the exclusive power of MOFERT, has been expanded to include a wide variety of economic zone directorates and many public and private enterprises. In addition China's economic and business bureaucracy is in flux. Though China has an image of a highly organized state, the roles of agencies are poorly defined and clashes of authority frequent. For example, it would be typical for a Chinese power company to delay installation of electricity to a newly built housing complex until some of its employees receive allocations of new apartments. If they can treat each other this way think how they can deal with you.

Chinese Negotiating Teams: Goals and Composition

Chinese negotiating goals are tied more to national policy than ours. Such Chinese aims include desires to satisfy consumer demands, acquire modern military and industrial technologies, build trade surpluses by producing quality export goods, and import raw materials or products not available in China. The composition of the Chinese team is likely to reflect this concern. Members with nominal private-sector titles, such as cost accountant, manager, or broker, may well be government officials.

The typical Chinese negotiating team, unlike its American counterpart, lacks lawyers. Instead it is likely to include a Communist Party official, MOFERT or special economic zone administrators, technical experts, budget specialists, bargaining tacticians, and representatives for the end user. If foreign exchange approval is involved there will be a representative of the Bank of China. Though all of these Chinese will be high in rank, their decisions will have to be validated at an even higher level. The person with the ultimate decision-making power is not likely to be present at the negotiations. Chinese prefer it this way.

At the other end of the spectrum, implementation of an agreement is likely to be the responsibility of a lower ranking individual, probably the person charged with direct control of the budget. Without the support of this person the agreement may be in your favor but there will be no implementation.

All of the members of the Chinese team will have different goals. This can be used in your favor. The foreign trade corporation or special zone administrators will be mainly concerned with prices and payments. The end user will focus on technical aspects related to performance. This person will possess considerable power. Budget people will be interested in foreign currency needs and chances for approval of the agreement by the Bank of China.

The Chinese will see your firm as a potential source for technology, data, and training. You might look at the Chinese side as a market for technology products and a source of cheap labor.

If countertrade is involved the approval ladder will be horizontal as well as vertical. You will need a three-way deal between your firm and two Chinese entities. This will be difficult due to notoriously poor coordination between Chinese organizations. If you are dealing with two Chinese agencies simultaneously and you notice abrasive sparks flying between them it might be time to break off negotiations. Such vendettas can last for decades.

Structuring Your Negotiating Team

The size of your team will vary with the scale of your project. In a smaller negotiation some members might be responsible for several duties.

Chinese do not believe young people possess the maturity and stability for responsible positions. Since they respect age and status, the leader of your delegation should ideally be past sixty and hold an important title. The higher the rank of your leader, the higher the rank of the Chinese leader. If both are high, more might be achieved. It might be desirable for your team leader to stay in China after the contract is signed in order to start up your operation and ensure the agreement is implemented. During the negotiations your leader will have certain ceremonial functions such as introducing your members to the Chinese side.

Since your business in China is likely to begin with an invitation to make a technical presentation, selection of your technical representative is critical. Choose someone who can clearly explain the capabilities and limitations of your product or service without divulging too much proprietary information.

Either your corporate lawyer or outside counsel might serve as your legal representative. Lists of attorneys who specialize in foreign law may be obtained from the International Trade Administration, Department of Commerce. This person should be familiar with Chinese business regulations and American corrupt practices law concerning bribery of foreign officials.

Some American negotiating teams designate a speaker and a listener. This ensures that every statement from the Chinese side is noted and that the American team speaks with one voice.

You will need a 1ogistics coordinator responsible for materials, travel, and communication. This will involve arrangement of visas and airline, hotel, and restaurant reservations. This person should take charge of assignment, purchase, and maintenance of all materials: typewriters, telex machines, computers, flip charts, projectors, extension cords, gifts, and business cards. Movement of all team property through customs is part of this assignment. Adapters and prongs will be needed to use American equipment on China's 220 volt, 50 cycle electrical system. These can be purchased in Hong Kong. You might also bring a VCR player to show the Chinese your home operation. Remember one picture is worth a thousand words!

The logistics coordinator might also serve as an advance person arriving in China a few days early to check hotel, travel, and restaurant reservations, ensure arrival of materials and mail, and go over the itinerary with the Chinese side.

The translator will be a key member. This person should also serve as cultural adviser and public relations director. You will need to make this person familiar with the details of your project. Though translators cost less in China than in the United States, some companies prefer to keep translators on their staffs. Others hire doctoral candidates in Chinese language or history. It takes about three years of intensive study to become a capable Chinese translator.

The translator/cultural adviser/public relations director should conduct cultural and language seminars for the team. This should involve practice in showing deference to the senior member of your team, which will be a pleasant change for that person. In rehearsals team members can practice showing respect for status based on age or position and addressing people by titles such as Manager Chao or President Wang. Training should emphasize practice in keeping emotions cool and responses slow. Learning even a little Mandarin can develop sensitivity for Chinese thought processes and aid basic communication. The Chinese side will appreciate interest in their language and culture.

Getting to Know You

One of the first decisions in the getting-to-know-you process involves whether to use an intermediary. In a nation where everyone is afraid of losing face intermediaries not only broker business deals but help people pick spouses, rent apartments, obtain employment, arbitrate disputes, and buy scarce items. You might want to hire an intermediary who could join your new operation after the close of negotiations. A good intermediary must be a paragon of virtue: sufficiently devious to save face for everyone, greedy enough to take money from both sides, sensitive to the nuances of a business deal, skilled in dealing with bureaucrats, and strong enough to endure hearing his compatriots call him a "foreign toady" without shedding tears.

The getting-to-know-you phase is important for obtaining information as well as connections. Since the Chinese government promulgates little information, you will have to dig for it. Before beginning active bargaining you will want to learn what the Chinese want and who makes the decisions. Can they deliver on promises? Are they minimizing their requirements? How are their options and actions limited by government policies? Your bottom line is the truth.

Banquets will be part of the familiarization process. For Chinese, food has a high priority. The standard greeting is "Have you eaten?" Delicious dishes are more important to Chinese than ambiance. During the three years I lived in Taipei, the best restaurant was seldom visited by tourists because it had cracked plaster walls and dirty floors strewn with spit-out pumpkin seeds. Yet the food was gourmet by any world standard.

At banquets the host is seated facing the door and the guest of honor sits at the host's right, a tradition originally established so they could be first to see invading swordsmen. The host should escort the guest of honor to the table. Whether in a restaurant or home, never refuse a course. Sea slugs and fish stomachs are considered delicacies. Eyeballs and brains may be reserved for you, the guest of honor. If you do not wish to eat something because it is staring back at you, use your chopsticks to move it around your plate. Mix it with other delicacies so it looks like you have sampled it. Thus, cook, host, and guest can all smile and save face.

You should hold the rice bowl close to your mouth and shove the rice toward you with chopsticks. Discarded food, such as bones and seeds, can be left on the table. You can show appreciation of the meal by belching but you must not blow your nose at the table. Business is seldom discussed over meals. Chinese usually do not dawdle after dining. They leave almost immediately.

Verbal Communication

Word choices in conversation should consider connotation as well as denotation of words. All verbal communication is heavily laden with cultural meanings. English, written left to right in cursive fashion, is as direct as our culture. Chinese, written from top to bottom, left to right, and right to left in many styles of strokes resembles painting. Characters have subtle shades of meaning and sometimes the manner of writing is as important as the content. Much of this extends from written to spoken communication. For Chinese, communication, like thought, is slower and more contemplative.

There are no direct translations between languages. "Father" in both English and Chinese has the same definition. But a father in China deserves great respect. In contrast a father in America can be an object for a child's rebellion. "Evaluation" in English translates as "self-criticism" in Chinese.

For better verbal communication speak slowly and avoid vague words and slang.

Nonverbal Communication

Silent communication is vital in bargaining. It begins by dressing more formally and conservatively than in the United States. This shows sincerity. In China people usually stand closer to others than in the United States. To beckon others extend your arm and hand, palm down, and flutter your fingers. When sitting place your hands in your lap. Keep your feet flat on the floor. To wink is rude.

Eye contact is fraught with nonverbal meanings. Chinese who are roughly equal maintain direct eye contact. A Chinese suffering admonishment from a superior avoids eye contact to show penitence. Even in routine situations a subordinate limits eye contact with a superior.

Informal behavior indicates disrespect to Chinese. So do not put your feet up on a chair or loosen your tie. Show you are serious by displaying restraint and keeping a straight face. If you exhibit a quick temper and act excitable Chinese will think you are childish. With them fast-talking sales types go down in flames. They value composure and dignity.

You need to keep all your antennae up for nonverbal clues, especially when the topic under discussion is awkward or embarrassing.

Tea

Tea plays an important part in Chinese business. The teahouse, just as the coffee house in Boswell's mercantile England, was a center for commercial contacts. The serving of tea is still a part of business. The most expensive tea is said to possess medicinal qualities. The cheapest "tea," consumed by poor people, is simply hot water. They call it "plain tea." Whether expensive or plain the boiling of water for tea prevents much disease.

Bribes and Gifts

How does a nation of one and a quarter billion people do business? The answer: connections. What helps make connections? The answer: gifts and bribes.

Since most forms of bribery are against U.S. law for American citizens, you will need the advice of your attorney. This section simply describes how the Chinese do it.

In China gifts and bribes are forms of etiquette essential to business. Chinese commerce is based on personal relationships established and maintained by giving and receiving gifts and bribes. Without such payments business would be more difficult and civil servants would starve. In China bribery becomes corrupt only when it exceeds the cultural norm. Everyone pays, not just to buy and sell but to get a tooth or tire fixed. When Chinese television crews or print journalists attend corporate news conferences, they leave with envelopes stuffed with money. Front pages of some Chinese papers are sold for as much as a quarter of a million dollars per day.

Check your attorney about business to business gifts which can often be legal.

Bribery can be frustrating to Westerners especially when it fails. An American machine-tool salesman I met at the bar of the Peace Hotel in Shanghai, crying in his Tsingtao beer, summarized this in slurred syllables: "In China you can't win even when you pay bribes."

Sexual Entertainment

During the Mao era China was puritanical about sex. Now attitudes are changing. If invited to sexual entertainment such as erotic shows by all means go. Leave your wife at the hotel. This is a necessary part of the Asian getting-to-know-you process. But do not accept sexual *services* paid by your host or counterpart. This is business not moral advice. For centuries Chinese negotiators have provided these services to ensure Westerners arrive at the bargaining table physically exhausted, mentally distracted, morally vulnerable, and socially indebted. Such practices are more likely in Hong Kong and Guangdong.

Face

In negotiating with Chinese, "yes" means "maybe," "maybe" means "no," and "no" is never spoken. If you hear a neutral response, "We will get back to you!" it might be time to pack your bags.

The Technical Meeting

Early in negotiations the Chinese will schedule a technical meeting. They will want to evaluate the technical expertise of your firm before deciding whether to continue negotiations.

You will find your counterparts thoroughly prepared. They will ask detailed questions and want to analyze the performance of your product or service under Chinese field conditions. They are likely to prefer to license your technology in order to upgrade existing plants rather than purchase turnkey operations.

Before the technical meeting you should determine your limits on divulging proprietary information. If your Chinese counterparts ask for "complete" data on your technology before licensing, be sure you protect your industrial and intellectual property rights.

Concept of Time

Chinese do not liked to be rushed. Chinese culture took five thousand years to develop, so be prepared for slow negotiations. Expect long introductions, endless lunches, frequent breaks for naps, refreshments, and slow sightseeing tours through the countryside.

Expect tough well-prepared adversaries who will be patient and leave no stone unturned. Time is not "of the essence" in China. If you have a need to add to your bottom line within three months, it will mean nothing to them. Chinese call this "quarterly myopia." It could take as long as three years to close a contract on a major project. Even then much might remain to negotiate.

The Contract

Little by little the form of an agreement should take shape, as in the accretion of colored dots in a pointillist painting.

Chinese negotiators, partly to avoid confrontation, tend to leave difficult areas to work themselves out after signing of the contract. Resist this. Require agreement on key details before anything is signed. Ask hard questions: What rate of exchange? Who has hiring authority? What will be done if raw materials or capital run out?

Be precise about conditions, definitions, and guarantees. Your Chinese counterparts will inevitably interpret the contract differently.

Finally, make plans to maintain contact with the other side after the contract is signed. Though Chinese tend to honor contracts and interpret them strictly, *guanxi* may ultimately be more important.

9. How To Get Help

Sources of Help

Much help is available for American firms seeking to do business with China. Sources of help include Chinese government agencies located in China and the United States, U.S. government agencies here and in China, and private enterprises in China and the United States.

Many American firms seem reluctant to use help available from our government. Perhaps they fear red tape. Yet the information and services available from the U.S. government are timely, thoroughly researched, and often free.

Addresses of agencies and firms mentioned here are listed in Chapter Thirteen.

U.S. GOVERNMENT AGENCIES

The International Trade Administration

The International Trade Administration, an agency of the Department of Commerce, is organized into trade development sections specializing in such industry sectors as capital goods, consumer goods, transportation, and industrial goods and services. Its staff includes experts on China. The International Trade Administration offers assistance ranging from export mailing lists to product marketing services.

The United States Foreign Commercial Service is an arm of the International Trade Administration. It was created to help American exports by assisting American businesses.

The Department of Commerce

The Department of Commerce has a marketing manager for China who assists American firms. Commerce publishes *Market Share Reports* which describe foreign markets. Its Office of Major Contracts assists U.S. firms in obtaining large foreign contracts. *World Data Reports* provides credit information on about two hundred thousand foreign firms. Statistical data on trade with China is detailed in reports titled *United States Trade with Major Trading Partners*. Many Commerce reports are now available on computer disks available at major libraries.

The Agency for International Development

The Agency for International Development provides feasibility funding for trade contracts and investments abroad. It also supports banks which finance joint American and foreign ventures.

The Export-Import Bank

The Export-Import Bank develops America's export potential by encouraging small and medium-sized businesses. It offers an array of loans, guarantees, and insurance programs. The Foreign Credit Insurance Corporation acts as an agent for the Export-Import Bank to insure American exporters against non-payment by foreign buyers.

The Overseas Private Investment Corporation

The Overseas Private Investment Corporation is the key federal agency for encouragement of American business investment in developing nations such as China. It furnishes feasibility funding, sponsors investment and trade missions, and provides insurance for currency convertibility, expropriation, war, and revolution. Direct loans and guarantees are also available. This corporation publishes *Washington's Best Kept Secrets: A U.S. Guide to International Business.*

The Small Business Administration

The Small Business Administration guarantees export financing and is structured to meet the needs of the small business owner who plans to enter export markets for the first time. The SBA operates both management and financial assistance programs. It helps connect American exporters with foreign buyers.

The State Department

The State Department publishes bulletins which provide market leads. State's Office of Business and Export Affairs publishes information on strategies and risk evaluation for American businesses considering foreign operations.

Library of Congress

The Library of Congress maintains a special section devoted to foreign laws.

U.S. Embassy and Consulates in China

The U.S. Embassy and consulates in China, through the office of the U.S. Trade Representative, provide feasibility funding for trade, contracts, and investments in China. They also publish information on commercial treaties and trade problems. The Foreign Commercial Service provides industry analyses, counsels American businesses, and provides financial information on Chinese businesses including potential partners. The economic section provides information on the Chinese economy and the Foreign Agricultural Service furnishes data on Chinese agriculture.

The U.S.-China Business Center of Shenzhen

The U.S.-China Business Center of Shenzhen, a joint effort between the Foreign Commercial Service of the U.S. Consulate in Guangzhou and the Shenzhen Information Center of the Shenzhen Municipal Government, opened in February 1993. Its purpose is to help American and Chinese businesses work with each other, often as joint venture partners. This center is only an hour by train from Hong Kong. For standard fees it offers a full range of services such as arranging contacts, making appointments, providing interpreters, organizing seminars, and servicing exhibitions. I visited this center and was impressed by the high quality of the English-speaking staff and the timeliness of their information.

Local Government Agencies

More and more states, counties, and cities are developing programs designed to assist firms in international business. Many state and local governments now sponsor trade missions to China.

PRIVATE AMERICAN ORGANIZATIONS

Dun and Bradstreet

Dun and Bradstreet issues *Private International Businesses* which lists credit information on over fifty thousand firms in over a hundred nations.

U.S. Attorneys Specializing in Foreign Law

A list of attorneys who specialize in foreign law may be obtained from the International Trade Administration, Department of Commerce.

Chamber of Commerce

American Chambers of Commerce in China such as ANCHAM in Hong Kong can provide comprehensive and up-to-date business information.

Banks

American banks provide a variety of services for firms planning to do business in China. Most have contacts in China. International development agencies such as the World Bank and Asian Development Bank are not merely lenders of billions of dollars. They buy engineering and contracting services for many of their projects. The International Monetary Fund can provide risk analyses for overseas markets.

Trading Companies

A 1982 American law allows formation of trading companies. For this purpose some provisions of antitrust laws are nullified. Check with your attorney and the International Trade Administration which provides information on exemptions and help in finding other firms interested in forming trading companies. The activities of trading companies are quite diverse, from structuring countertrades to providing finance.

Training Programs

There are some excellent short programs designed to prepare American executives for the cultural and business challenges of China. Prominent among these are BCIU at American University in Washington, D.C., and Business Programs of the East-West Center in Honolulu.

Language orientation is also available. The Pacific International Language School in Honolulu offers short courses in

Mandarin. Many American corporations send executives to Hawaii for language study prior to assignment to China.

Relocation and Orientation Companies

Many relocation companies offer cultural as well as moving services. International Orientation Services of Northbrook, Illinois, has one of the best staffs in the business. The professional organization for intercultural training, education, and research is SIETAR International based in Washington, D.C.

CHINESE ORGANIZATIONS

Chinese Embassy and Consulates in the United States

The Chinese Embassy and consulates in the United States can be good starting points for establishing appropriate contacts.

Ministry of Foreign Economic Relations and Trade (MOFERT)

MOFERT and its foreign trade corporations (FTCs) are probably the most important trade and investment agencies in China. MOFERT is organized to trade by commodity or product.

Special Zone Administrations

China has a variety of special zones, provincial centers, and independent municipalities permitted to trade. Trade by private factories and individuals is gradually growing.

PART THREE

The Personal Experience

This book is not intended to be a tourist guide but this section should increase your enjoyment of China.

Much of your business effectiveness will depend upon how well you adjust to China at a personal level. Thus there will be considerable overlap between your personal and business activities.

The more you enjoy China and its people the more success you will have in your business endeavors.

10. Travel Tips

Passports and Visas

A U.S. passport and Chinese visa are required to enter China. Tourist visas, valid for thirty-day visits, are good for six months from date of approval. Multiple-entry visas (good for more than two entries) are limited to business people invited by a Chinese agency or enterprise.

Chinese visas may be obtained at the Embassy of the People's Republic of China in Washington, D.C., or from Chinese consulates in the United States or abroad.

At present no visa is required for American passport holders to enter Hong Kong for up to thirty days. Presumably a Chinese visa will be needed to enter Hong Kong after it reverts to China.

Timing the Visit

For comfort fall is the best time. In the summer heat and humidity, particularly in southern China, can be debilitating. Northern China is bitterly cold in the winter. South of the Yangze River buildings are seldom heated no matter how cold. Though Hong Kong and Guangzhou are in the same latitude as Hawaii and Calcutta, they are not tropical. Winters are chilly. Bring warm sweaters and coats. Dress in layers.

Packing

Business suits and dresses are standard for northern China. Short-sleeved white shirts and slacks are acceptable in the south. If you have a tight itinerary bring at least one set of drip-dry clothes and soap. Other useful items include toilet paper, antiseptic, antacid, aspirins, diarrhea and cold medicines, and insect repellent. Long bus, train, and boat trips can be more pleasant by bringing a collapsible cup, hand towel, chopsticks, water flask and can opener. Prescription medicines should be kept in their original vials.

Jet Lag

Your flight from the West Coast to China will take about a dozen hours. During your westward journey you will gain many hours but lose a day when your plane crosses the International Date Line.

Unfortunately you will not be able to reset your mind and body as easily as your watch. Dozens of physical and emotional problems will arise. Your pulse, heartbeat, blood pressure, temperature, liver and kidney functions and many hormonal balances will go awry. Symptoms of jet lag can include confusion, distorted vision, stiff muscles, memory loss, nervousness and sweating. At your first negotiating meeting in China your body might be tuned to three in the morning.

Jet lag can not be avoided but it can be reduced. Eat light, regular, nutritious meals before and during the flight. Avoid alcohol and caffeine. Drink plenty of water and fruit juice. Walk the aisles of your aircraft. A few days before departure, try to adjust your meals and sleep periods to the time at your destination. Take comfort items such as eyewash and cold cream with you on the plane.

Arrival

Chinese Customs procedures will include passport and visa clearance, customs and currency declarations, and health checks. Inoculations are only required if arriving from an infected area. But it is a good idea to keep shots current.

Customs allows foreigners to bring in six hundred cigarettes, two liters of liquors and one pint of perfume without payment of duties. All valuables should be declared. Typical items prohibited include opium, explosives, lottery tickets and similar articles not normally used in business. Chinese currency may not be taken in or out of the country.

Expect anything from Chinese Customs. Arriving in Shanghai by boat from Hong Kong, I was pulled out of line and placed in a small holding room by two mean-looking officials armed with pistols and pock-marked faces. I had committed no crime. But I could already feel bamboo slivers under my fingernails and was composing a confession which I hoped would be acceptable. The interrogation began: "Please explain the meaning of 'so long.'" They simply wanted a free English lesson. We became friends. Did Confucius say something about the agonies of overactive imaginations?

Money

Change a minimum of money at the point of entry. Banks and hotels in town usually pay better rates. Credit card and traveler's check exchange transactions are usually more favorable than cash for cash.

There are automatic teller machines in Hong Kong which dispense cash through insertion of major credit cards. Most credit cards are accepted in Hong Kong and use is expanding on the mainland.

When you enter China you will be asked to declare your currency and traveler's checks. You should keep a copy of this declaration and all currency exchange receipts since you may have to show these to change Chinese currency back to dollars. The Chinese dollar is called a yuan; the dime, a mao; the penny, a fen. *Kuai* is a classifier used when speaking of sums.

In southern China Hong Kong dollars are in great demand.

China International Travel Service (CITS)

CITS is the government agency charged with making travel arrangements for foreigners. There have been many complaints against CITS regarding high prices and unsure service. With more experience in a market economy CITS will likely improve.

Electricity

Most Chinese electricity is 220 volt, 50 cycle, single phase. You will need transformers and three-prong flat plugs to use personal appliances and business equipment. Some hotels can furnish these. They may also be purchased in Hong Kong.

Time

All China is on Beijing time, thirteen hours ahead of Eastern Standard Time in the United States.

Chinese business hours are usually from eight A.M. to noon and two to six P.M. Monday through Friday and eight A.M. to noon on Saturdays. Most shops are open from nine A.M. to seven P.M. every day.

Tipping

Tipping is not a Chinese custom. Most restaurants have a ten per cent service charge. You should leave small coins from the change. Do not tip taxi drivers. A tip should be reserved for unusual services such as a hotel porter carrying heavy baggage.

You may have to pay an inducement to get some people to do what they should be doing. In such cases a "tip" is given before the service is rendered, not after. This system, involving an etiquette for bribery, extends to tourists as well as business people. I usually carry U.S. coins and one dollar bills as "souvenirs" for this purpose. American pens, cigarettes, and one-ounce liquor bottles will also do the job.

Getting Around

China has many new regional airlines. Air travel is expanding too rapidly for proper maintenance and training. Old Soviet planes parked in paddies for decades are back in service. Mechanical devices are relatively new to China. The typical Chinese idea of maintenance is to use a machine until it stops working.

There is a legendary story about a Chinese flight crew which inadvertantly locked itself out of the cockpit while visiting the washroom at the back of the plane. At thirty thousand feet the plane, flying on automatic pilot, hit rough air and began bouncing. Oblivious to the shrieks of the passengers, the crew finally gained entrance to the cockpit by demolishing the door with a fire axe.

Chinese airlines usually will not confirm reservations until the night before the flight.

Chinese aircraft accidents are seldom reported in the press. The exception occurs when a foreigner is a victim.

China has four classes of trains: soft sleeper, soft seat, hard sleeper, and hard seat. Reservations must be made for a specific seat or bed as well as the train. Otherwise you might end up on the floor. Be sure your car displays a sign showing your destination. Cars are sometimes left on spurs to be picked up by other trains. Failure to check the sign could cause you to wake up on the trans-Siberian railway. Loudspeakers in many cars blare night and day. These can easily be sabotaged with a pair of pliers so bring one.

Going by bus provides ample opportunity to see scenery. Many buses are rickety so you will have extra time to sightsee while they stop for repairs. Bring earplugs. Buses always honk because only honking buses have the right of way.

Boats are best. Purchase of tickets is easier. There is room to move about. Usually the food is good, the cabins clean, the crews friendly. I took a voyage on the *Hai Hwa* from Hong Kong to Shanghai. Each morning the Chinese practiced tai chi on deck to classical Chinese music as the sun rose over the East China Sea. I recommend this for people interested in informal Chinese hospitality rather than plastic luxury. The address of China Merchants and Shipping Company is listed in Chapter Thirteen.

Many taxis lack meters. Set the price before entering and carry small bills. Cars with drivers are available to rent by the day. It is best to choose an older driver with a low performance car.

Health

Before leaving check your medical professional for immunizations: polio, tetanus, typhoid, cholera, yellow fever, hepatitis, encephalitis and influenza. Gamma globulin might help prevent hepatitis which is prevalent in China. Your doctor might recommend chloroquine or fansidar for malaria prevention.

Except in Hong Kong, never drink tap water. Chinese drink tea or hot water because boiling water destroys deadly germs. Boiled water in a thermos will be in your hotel room. Bottled water is readily available. If you visit rural areas (where some mines and factories are located), you might wish to bring water purification pills and your own chopsticks. I have seen Chinese pull towels from their pockets to clean chopsticks in restaurants. They can carry hepatitis.

It is usually safe to eat Chinese food hot from the wok. Fruits and vegetables which have skin are safe to eat if you peel them yourself. Avoid foods exposed to flies or dust. If you eat at street stalls or carts go early and patronize busy ones. The food will have less time to spoil. Except in the best restaurants, never eat cold salads or desserts, unbottled juice drinks, ice cream, or dairy products. Do not assume ice is safe. It might be made from unboiled water or have been handled carelessly.

Asian squat toilets offer no place to sit. Secure your keys, wallets, and other valuables so they do not fall in the smelly abyss. Squatting is rough on the knees. Some Asian experts practice squats to build knee muscles before leaving.

Safety

China has very little violent crime but theft, particularly in Guangzhou, is rampant. Do not flash big bills or appear vulnerable. Passports, big bills and other valuables should be carried under your clothes, in pouches suspended from your neck or attached to your belt. Keep a throwaway wallet you can afford to lose to a thief. Mine contains Monopoly money and my library card.

Departure and Return

Your airline will want you to confirm your reservation well in advance and arrive at the airport several hours early. If you depart China on Air China, the nation's flagship carrier, be sure not to miss the plane. Its penalties are more stringent than most airlines.

When changing Chinese or Hong Kong money back to U.S. dollars at the departure airport, save twenty dollars or so in local currency for snacks while waiting and departure tax. Keep all items you declared on arrival in the same bag so you can easily show them to customs upon departure. Be sure you have receipts for all purchases.

When you return to the United States, customs will allow four hundred dollars in goods duty-free. If you have been outside the United States more than thirty-one days this increases. Beyond this regulations get complicated. It is best to contact customs before leaving if you expect to exceed these limits.

11. Living in China

Inflation Warning

There has been considerable inflation. Expect to spend more than indicated in all but the most recent guidebooks. Current costs can be obtained from sources listed in Chapter 13.

Moving and Arrival

Your move to China will be a major project. Many American firms will hire a relocation company to process travel documents, ship household goods, meet customs requirements, find housing, and arrange school enrollment for children. A good relocation company can save more than it costs.

Do not pack for shipment items you will need during your trip and while waiting for your goods. While you are settling your finances, save some time to check your car, health, and house insurance, cancel utilities, and obtain an international driver's license.

Cultural Shock

In the past many American business people avoided cultural shock by avoiding China. They kept to their enclaves and limited involvement to managing Chinese employees and servants (for which they paid too little) and buying Chinese curios (for which they paid too much).

Times have changed. China has come into its own right. If you want to deal with it, you will have to get involved and undergo the tunnel called cultural shock. You will not suffer from it immediately upon your arrival in China. It takes a while to get the disease. The symptoms will appear when you realize you are not a tourist but someone who will have to live as a foreigner in a strange environment. As soon as your initial enthusiasm for everything Chinese wears off, you will feel considerable frustration and irritation due to difficulties with food, weather, customs, language, and manners. You might give up and go home.

Your business success will depend largely on your personal adjustment. To contribute to your company's China venture you will have to break out of your Western shell. You will have to learn something about Chinese culture, economics, business, politics, and language. You can prepare for this by enrolling in the language and business courses listed in the address chapter.

Housing and Schools

Housing and schools cost more than in the United States. Hong Kong has the highest prices. Housing in Zhuhai and Shenzhen, which are only an hour away from Hong Kong are about a third less. Even Shanghai is expensive. A French electronics engineer told me she and her husband paid three thousand dollars per month to rent a small apartment.

In the past the Chinese government assigned housing to foreigners. Now foreigners are free to choose their own apartments, villas, and hotels. Many rent in new towns which are springing up in major Chinese cities. Shanghai's Hongqiao New Town is an example. This is a carefully planned community which integrates residential, commercial, and recreational functions at Western standards.

There are many considerations in renting housing besides costs. What is the availability of electric and phone services? Is there a community guard system? Are groceries and foreign schools convenient? Is a car needed? Are taxis and buses nearby? Does the buiding have storage rooms and an emergency water supply? How far is it from the airport?

There are American, British, or Hong Kong schools in most major cities of China. Tuition is higher than similar schools in the United States. A Dutch petrochemical executive told me he paid twelve hundred dollars a month tuition for his daughter for enrollment in a Hong Kong kindergarten in Shanghai.

Servants

Most expatriates employ one or more servants as maids, cooks, gardeners, guards, or drivers. Families with several children sometimes have more than one maid. Probably the best way to obtain a household servant is from another Westerner who is returning to the United States. Then you will likely get an employee who is honest, reliable, and trained in Western ways. Servants are cheap. Matters such as salary reviews, bonuses, health exams, room and board, holidays, vacations, and termination pay should be settled at the time of hiring.

Most Americans have no experience with servants. Some will find them to be invasions of privacy. Your cook might object if you putter around in the kitchen. Your amah will probably spoil your children.

Radio, Television, Film

Radio, television, and film are available in English. CNN and other international news programs are present in China.

Censorship takes a variety of forms. A German injection molding salesman in Shanghai told me a local cadre had ordered him to remove his satellite dish. Only hotels and large apartment complexes are now allowed these devices.

The Chinese government halted showing of the film, *Farewell to My Concubine*, which won honors at the Cannes

International Film Festival, after only two showings in Shanghai. This film offered an unvarnished portrayal of modern Chinese life which was too much for the government.

Postal, Telephone, Telex

Mail service from China to the United States is fast and reliable for people living in a specific location in China but slow for someone moving from place to place. Messages announcing mail are likely to be lost or poorly translated. Packages to the United States must be inspected unsealed by customs officers who are available only at the larger post offices. Regulation packing materials and customs forms must be used. Airmail letters from China to the United States take roughly a week for delivery.

Telephone, telex, and fax services are available from business centers in hotels. Service is dependable but may take time. Deluxe hotels offer direct dial service to the United States.

Newspapers

Newspapers in English are available in most major Chinese cities. *The South China Morning Post* is the major English language paper in Hong Kong. After 1997 this paper could be singled out by Beijing because of its independent editorial policies. In the best Western journalistic tradition it reports the dark as well as the bright sides of life in China. The only nationwide English language newspaper in China, *The China Daily*, also tries to follow a policy of objective and open reporting.

Health

One should always drink boiled water. Tap water is safe when it leaves the pumping station but picks up polluted ground water through leaks in pipes when excessive demand creates a vacuum.

Hospitals with Western standards are available in China's larger cities. Some are listed in the address chapter. Medical care in China is not free. It is a good idea to keep your shots current. Be prepared for medical emergencies. Global Assist, a program of American Express, can be very helpful.

Except in the best restaurants try to eat food hot off the wok. One should also try to avoid salads and dairy foods. Your common sense should serve you well.

Reverse Cultural Shock

You will likely experience reverse cultural shock upon your return to the United States. This might be severe if there has been substantial social change during your absence. My family and I were in Asia during the American cultural revolution of the 1960s. We returned to the United States of the 1970s with 1950s habits, ideas, and values, strangers in our own land.

American society is probably the most dynamic in the world. If you keep track of recent developments by reading American magazines and talking with newly arrived Americans, you will lessen the impact of reverse cultural shock upon your return to the United States.

Surprises

Living in China will be uncomfortable at times, particularly when business takes you to rural areas. But life in China will seldom be boring. Anything can happen.

Be prepared for food surprises. In Shanghai I ate live shrimp, a local specialty. Their legs wiggle when they are crunched between teeth but they are undoubtedly fresh. I stopped when one escaped for a swim in my stomach. Next time I will order something else such as the soup of boiled chicken feet which cured my upset stomach in Guangzhou.

My hotel in Xiamen had signs forbidding some traditional Chinese customs: "No birds allowed in the rooms. No firework explosions in the halls."

I had always wondered how Chinese sing since tones are essential to give meaning to the spoken language. Changing tones to follow melodies removes meaning. So I asked a Chinese baritone. His answer: "We simply forget the tones!"

While walking through a subway pedestrian crossing in Shanghai, I observed dozens of office workers enjoying the lunch break by practicing tangos, foxtrots, and waltzes to taped music. Enjoying their human rights, they had no fear of being mugged.

12. Things To Do, See, and Learn

New Perspectives

You will do better business if you crack out of your Western shell and actively participate in the life of China. Firsthand experiences will provide you valuable new perspectives and insights. Think of travel as a process of gathering infinite horizons.

China offers a human model most different from ours, one developed during five thousand years of isolation from the rest of the world. Sieze the opportunity to see customs, taste flavors, smell odors, and hear sounds which are authentic antiques.

Imbibe here from a few wellsprings bubbling with the essence of China.

Hong Kong

One's plane alights on a carpet of glittering neon. Kai Tak's runway extends far out in the harbor amid bobbing junks and sampans.

Hong Kong is compact and easy to see. All the modern enjoyments await: dining, shopping, sightseeing, horseracing, golfing, swimming, and boating. There is much to see: Aberdeen, Stanley Market, Repulse Bay, the Art and Space Museums, Ocean Park, the Star Ferries, and the Sung Dynasty Village. The Mass Transit Railway connects most attractions.

One can rise above it all by boarding the funicular tram for a ride to the top of Victoria Peak. Before air conditioning mold grew overnight on belts and shoes and lung ailments were common. To escape the damp heat people hired coolies to carry them in chairs to the top of the Peak, highest of a hundred hills, where cool breezes blow in from the sea.

During the revolutions on the mainland much religious tradition was destroyed. Through it all Hong Kong kept the faith. Over 350 Buddhist and Taoist temples are scattered over the hills. When the din of urban Hong Kong becomes too much, visit one for a quiet interlude. It is the custom upon entering to walk to the left of the big bowl of burning incense. Purchase of a few sticks of incense or a small curio is appreciated. The colors of the temples have meaning: green for peace and eternity, gold for wealth and power, red for happiness.

Guangzhou (Canton) and Guangdong Province

Consumers here, induced by Hong Kong television, have developed tastes for such goods as compact disks, fashion sneakers and cognac. The streets are lined with shops selling consumer goods: refrigerators, washing machines, motorcycles and electronic gadgets. Marxism is irrelevant. Rooms formerly devoted to Communist meetings are used for commercial offices, auctions, and fashion shows.

The spirit of Guangzhou's business past resides at Whompoa, a harbor a few miles down the Pearl River. Here the Chinese government required European ships to anchor in order to keep their sailors out of Canton. The anchorage is still filled with ships, white-winged junks with pendulum masts swinging with rhythmic swells.

After the overthrow of the Qing Dynasty by the Nationalist Revolution of 1911, Whompoa became the site for a Chinese military academy established to produce officers to lead armies against northern warlords. Whompoa was electrified by the energy of young men destined for fame: Sun Yat-sen, father of Nationalist China; Chiang Kai-shek, Commandant; Mao Zedong and Zhou Enlai, political officers; and Ho Chi Minh, a Vietnamese colleague. These men dominate the history of East Asia in the twentieth century.

Today the influence of Guangdong Province continues. It hosts three special economic zones and is at the cutting edge of China's meteoric, economic expansion.

Xiamen

From my boat the first view of Xiamen (Amoy) revealed a range of hills encased in jade-green verdure, a veneer slick as lacquer. The voyage had been smooth and uneventful. How different from the turbulent Taiwan Straits of the 1960s! Then, as a young Marine major, I watched a squad of Nationalist frogmen disembark from a Chinese craft offshore. They were taking their final exam to qualify as Seals: swim to Xiamen, attend a movie, and bring back the ticket. The Chinese Civil War was then in full swing with daily artillery duels between Communist positions at Xiamen and Nationalist guns on Quemoy Island. Both sides rotated new recruits through the fire zone so they could experience that most sacred sacrament of war, baptism by fire. Capture of these frogmen would mean torture and death.

During the Mao era entry to Xiamen and the rest of the coast was restricted, even for Chinese. Revolutionary energy went into the interior. Economic growth in Xiamen's Special Economic Zone is now so rapid that parts of it look like the coast of Southern California. Xiamen's International Airport and large harbor are among China's best.

There are traditional sightseeing places: Gulang Island, Suzhuang Gardens (designed after the one in the classical novel, *Dream of the Red Chamber*), Nanputuo Temple, Wanshi Botanical Gardens (containing a redwood tree planted by Nixon), and beautiful beaches.

I climbed up Five Elders (Wulao) Peak in a driving downpour. Thunder burst from billowing black clouds. Forks of white fire raked the rain with incandescent flashes. At the top streams of sunlight suddenly appeared. Time seemed to slow to a rivulet. I could see great distances across the Taiwan Straits.

Later, in the calm residue of the storm, I swam off a picture-perfect white sand beach. In the Lujiang Channel an undertow as insistent as a Chinese host pulled me toward the East China Sea.

Shanghai

In Mandarin Shanghai means "over the sea." Far from it! The city is situated about a dozen miles up river on flat mud banks.

Shanghai, the largest city in Asia, is cosmopolitan in its tastes. The city has a sweet tooth, not only for candies but for the luscious products of world-class designers. Women spend freely on the freshest fashions in clothes and cosmetics. Even during the Cultural Revolution many wore Western hairdos. Such tastes originated over a century ago.

Visitors arriving by sea at the end of the nineteenth century were greeted by a magnificent European city, "the Paris of the East," resplendent with public parks, band concerts on summer evenings, and bright electric lights (the first in Asia) which burned all night. Here was one of the few Chinese cities with ice and plumbing. The International Settlement was divided into three parts: English, American, and French. Coolies were required to grease the wheels of their rickshaws so gentlemen at their clubs could conduct business in quiet. River traffic was stopped for the sailing of the regatta. Polo and cricket clubs enjoyed long voyages up the Yangze in lavish houseboats. In British Gardens a sign reading "No dogs or Chinese" resulted in hurt feelings.

Vestiges of this period still abound. Old European buildings still line the Bund, a British-Indian term for an embankment on a muddy shore. These imperial structures are such architectural treasures that I kept going back to see them. After the ravages of the Red Guards, they are being restored with explanatory placards describing each building's historical significance.

Shanghai kept its authentic art deco artifacts and views as it watched the changing pageant of history: occupation by Japan's rising sun, followed by liberation by the People's Army, the wilting of the Hundred Flowers, the excesses of the Great Leap Forward and the Cultural Revolution, and the advent of market-Leninism. The city even survived Mao's wife, Jiang Qing, who banned boat traffic on the Huangpu and Suzhou Rivers so she could sleep in quiet at Shanghai Mansions.

Shanghai benefitted from the Sui Dynasty's construction of the Grand Canal which united the Yangze and Yellow Rivers. Today one-third of China's trade passes through this confluence. On misty nights foghorns from foreign freighters reverberate across the water. On clear days malodorous industrial sulphur emissions well up from factories on the shore. People in Shanghai call these "yellow dragons."

At the Peace Hotel I watched a jazz band leader order wizened, eighty-year old musicians to play some Dixieland: "Take it away." The group had been formed at this hotel, the old Cathay, in the 1930s. Performances were interrupted during the Cultural Revolution because Red Guards crumpled them and their instruments. Long after this break, in the 1980s, the band again picked up the beat.

Decrepit Dixie and yellow dragons: so sad and strange, yet wonderful and transcendent. China endures!

My plane from Shanghai sailed south on a sea of sunshine. Below lay the China coast sweltering under rumpled sheets of white heat. Chasms in the clouds revealed a patchwork of manicured croplands, weathered ridges, and winding rivers, backdrops for a timeworn drama. Such gaps grant glimpses of China's soul: vast, imperishable, immutable.

Dining

Chinese cuisine reflects China's scarcities. Food fried quickly in a wok saves oil and fuel. There are many regional differences. Cantonese cooking is colorful and sweet. Fujian food stresses steamed and stewed dishes, particularly fish. Beijing and Shanghai dishes are mild; the first features duck and chicken; the second, seafood. Hunan's courses are hot; Sichuan's very hot. Sichuan people are pepper masochists who draw distinctions between peppers which burn, bite, and numb. Sichuan's seductive black peppers, tiny and vile, produce a joyful stinging pain which brings tears to the eyes. Peppers were first brought to China from Central America by Portuguese traders stationed at Macau.

In *dim sum* (*yum cha*) restaurants waiters circulate with carts containing savory viands such as shrimp dumplings, eggrolls, pot stickers, steamed buns, and a variety of sweet cakes. Diners select favorites. The bill is based on a count of the empty dishes at the end of the meal.

A walk through a Chinese food market can be an intense experience. Expect anything: haggling hags, wrinkled pickles, vast varieties of exotic fruits, fish thrashing in buckets, moon cakes first sold a thousand years ago, live snakes, dogs, cats, monkeys, eels, and turtles. In many restaurants these will be displayed in cages and tanks in the lobby. You pick your meal and it is killed in the kitchen. Chinese like food fresh.

Some culinary artists use unique ways to bring back customers. According to the Chinese press, cooks in more than a dozen provinces were caught flavoring their dishes with opium pods, a spice not very nice. Choose your meals carefully to avoid spending the rest of your life at a Chinese noodle stand!

Alcohol has always been an adjunct to Chinese meals. Rice wine, fermented in many grades, varieties, and proofs has been the traditional drink. Some liquors such as Mao Tai are very powerful. Myriad Chinese characters express subtle nuances of inebriation. In its long history China has had over forty prohibitions. All failed.

Shopping

Hong Kong is no longer bargain heaven. But it still offers a vast array of high quality, duty-free goods such as silks, gems, pearls, artifacts in ivory, gold, and jade; linen, cameras, electronics, watches, furniture, computers, tailored clothing, leather goods, and furs. Duties apply to alcohol, tobacco, perfumes, and cosmetics but these are low.

China now has a corner on sales of low-cost goods. A cornucopia awaits the serious shopper: cashmeres, jades, silks, porcelain, embroidery, and books. Chinese jade is so smooth it can only be described as suave.

In large stores, particularly those run by the government, prices are fixed. In smaller shops the ancient Chinese tradition of haggling is honored.

Some arts outlets look more like museums than stores. To leave China with an antique one must have a receipt from a government store. Some animal products may not be brought into the United States because they represent endangered species. Check with customs before leaving if you plan such purchases.

Sports

Since most Chinese live in crowded conditions they look forward to outings such as beach visits, picnics, hikes, and boating. Jogging is now a rage. The Shanghai marathon, held every March, is a national event.

Ping Pong, badminton, and basketball are popular because they take little room in a crowded country. Entire families can be seen skating, kiting, and swimming.

Golf courses, tennis courts, and swimming pools are available in major Chinese cities. Most hotels open their recreational facilities to visitors for a fee.

Hong Kong, thick with British tradition, provides international competition in tennis, squash, golf, rugby, and soccer.

Performing Arts

Movies are probably the most popular form of entertainment in China. "Movie" in Mandarin translates to "electric shadow." Chinese of all ages seem fascinated. Chinese academy awards go to kung fu flicks.

Productions in the fine arts range from Western and Chinese opera to concerts by rock bands. Hong Kong has a famous arts festival in the spring and fall. The Shanghai Music Festival is held every spring. Beijing is now a stop on the world concert circuit.

Things to Learn

Take advantage of the chance to learn about the world's oldest continuous culture. Many colleges and private schools offer Chinese language instruction to foreigners. Spoken Chinese, because it has so little grammar, can be easier to learn than many languages. Your first conversation with a Chinese in Mandarin will be a thrill. One can also learn Chinese cooking, calligraphy, shadowboxing, painting, palmistry, and herbal medicine.

Visiting an English Corner is a good way to meet local people. Chinese interested in practicing English gather at designated corners. A native speaker who shows up is an instant hero. Hotel clerks can usually tell you the time and location of English Corners. Such visits contributed to this book.

13. Useful Addresses

This chapter lists useful addresses and phone numbers. The purpose of the list is to help get you started. No attempt is made to include all addresses in a category. Listed hotels and restaurants are suitable for business purposes. Chinese telephone directories are available from the American Embassy, U.S. and Foreign Commercial Service, Beijing.

Banks

Bank of America
Union Building—Room 1802
100 Yanan East Road
Shanghai, PRC
Tel: 328-9661

Bank of China
137 Chang Ti
Guangzhou
Guangdong, PRC
Tel: 220543

Bank of China
415 Madison Ave.
New York, NY 10017
(212) 935-3101

Bank of China
Xijiaominxiang 17
Beijing, PRC
Tel: 338521

Bank of China
23 Zhongshan Rd.
Shanghai, PRC
Tel: 321-5666

Business Training Programs

American School of International Management
Glendale, Arizona, 85306
(602) 978-7011

Business Programs
East-West Center
1777 East-West Road
Honolulu, Hawaii 96848
(808) 944-7611

Business Training and Development Institute (BCIU)
Executive Programs—Suite 244
The American University
3301 New Mexico Avenue
Washington, D.C. 20016
(202) 686-2771

Chambers of Commerce (American) in China

AmCham in Beijing
Great Wall Sheraton Hotel
G/F, North Donghuan Ave.
Beijing 100026, PRC
Tel: (86-1) 500-5566 (x2271)

AmCham in Guangzhou
c/o U.S. Consul-General
12/F China Hotel Office Tower
Guangzhou, Guangdong, PRC
Tel: (86-20) 667-7842

AmCham in Shanghai
General Post Office Box 246
Shanghai, PRC

American Chamber of Commerce
(Hong Kong)
1030 Swire House, Hong Kong
Tel: 526-0165

Chinese Embassy and Consulates in the United States

Embassy of the People's
Republic of China
2300 Connecticut Ave. NW
Washington, D.C. 20008
(202) 328-2501

Consul-General
People's Republic of China
104 S. Michigan Ave.
Chicago, IL
(312) 346-0287

Consul-General
People's Republic of China
3417 Montrose
Houston, TX 77006
(713) 524-0778

Consul-General
People's Republic of China
501 Shatto Place—Ste #300
Los Angeles, CA 90020
(213) 380-2507

Consul-General
People's Republic of China
520 12th Ave.
New York, NY 10036
(212) 279-1270

Consul-General
People's Republic of China
1450 Laguna Street
San Francisco, CA 94115
(415) 573-4885

Chinese Government Agencies

Center for Introducing New
Products
CCPIT,
Box 1420
Beijing, PRC

China Council for Promotion
of International Trade
4 Fuxingmenwai Street
Beijing, PRC
Tel: 867229

China Council for the Promotion
of International Trade
41/F, China Resources Building
26 Harbour Drive
Wanchai, Hong Kong
Tel: 827-7038

Ministry of Foreign Economic
Relations and Trade (MOFERT)
Dongchangan Jie
Beijing, PRC
Tel: 553031

China United Trading Ltd.
One Penn Plaza, Suite 1915
250 West 34th Street
New York, NY 10119
(212) 947-3130

China International Trust
and Investment Corporation
CITIC Building
19 Jianguomenwai
Beijing, PR
Tel: 5002255

Hospitals

Beijing Medical College Hospital
1 Dong Shuafuyuan Hutong
Beijing, PRC
Tel: 553731

Shanghai No. 1 People's Hospital
190 Beisuzhou Lu
Shanghai, PRC
Tel: 324-1000

First People's Hospital of Guangzhou
Guangzhou, Guangdong
Tel: 886-421

Hotels

Beijing International
9 Jianguomenwai Ave.
Beijing, PRC
Tel: 512-6688

Holiday Inn Lido
Jichang Road
Beijing, PRC
Tel: 500-6688

Hot Springs Hotel
Central Wusi Road
Fuzhou, PRC
Tel: 551818

Lujiang Hotel
3 Haihou Road
Xiamen, PRC
Tel: 23235

Dongfang Hotel
120 Liu Hua Road
Guangzhou, PRC
Tel: 669900

Holiday Inn Center
Huanshi Dong Lu
Guangzhou, PRC
Tel: 766999

Hilton
2 Queen's Road
Central, Hong Kong
Tel: 525-3111

Mandarin Oriental
5 Connaught Road
Central, Hong Kong
Tel: 522-0111

Empress
17 Chatham Road
Tsimshatsui
Kowloon, Hong Kong
Tel: 366-0211

Hyatt Regency
67 Nathan Road
Tsimshatsui
Kowloon, Hong Kong
Tel: 311-1234

Garden Hotel
58 Maoming Rd.
Shanghai, PRC
Tel: 433-1111

Shanghai Hilton Intl.
250 Huashan Rd.
Shanghai, PRC
Tel: 255-0000

Joint U.S.-Chinese Business Office

United States-China Business
Center
No. 1, Tongxin Rd.—1st Floor
Shenzhen, Guangdong, PRC 518027
Tel: (86) (755) 2240056 x1012/1022

Language Services and Training

Pacific Rim Connections, Inc.
1838 El Camino Real #109
Burlingame, CA 94010
(415) 697-0911
(Language Software)

Pacific International Language
School
1451 King St.—Suite #404
Honolulu, Hawaii 96814
(808) 946-8485

Private American Organizations

U.S.-China Business Council
1818 N Street NW—Suite 500
Washington, D.C. 20036
(202) 429-0340, 828-8300

National Council for U.S.-
China Trade (China Office)
Room 1136—Peking Hotel
Beijing, PRC
Tel: 552231 x1136

National Council for U.S.-
China Trade (U.S. Office)
1050 Seventeenth St. NW #350
Washington, D.C. 20036
(202) 429-0340

Relocation, Consulting Services

Clarke Consulting Group, Inc.
Three Lagoon Drive—Ste #230
Redwood City, CA 94065
(415) 591-8100

International Orientation
Resources
707 Skokie Blvd. #350
Northbrook, IL 60062
(312) 205-0066

Restaurants

Cui Hua Lu
60 Wangfujing
Beijing, PRC
Tel: 554581

Tong He Ju
3 Xsi Nan Road
Beijing, PRC
Tel: 666-357

Nan Yuan
120 Qianjin Lu
Guangzhou, PRC
Tel: 550532

Dongfan
120 Liuhua Rd.
Guangzhou, PRC
Tel: 669900

Yangzhou
308 Nanjing Rd.
Shanghai, PRC
Tel: 322-2777

Xin Ya
719 Nanjing Rd.
Shanghai, PRC
Tel: 322-4393

Shipping Firm

China Merchants Shipping and
Enterprise Company
315 Des Voeux Road, Hong Kong
815-1006 or 850-5985

Special Economic Zones

Shantou SEZ Office
4/F, Foreign Trade Building
Yingchun Lu
Shantou, Guangdong, PRC

Shenzhen Economic Zone Admin.
2/F Luohu Building
Jianshe Rd.
Shenzhen, PRC

Shekou Development Zone
Nanshan, Shekou Industrial Area
Shenzhen SEZ, Guangdong, PRC

Xiamen SEZ Development Corp.
105 Xian Jie
Xiamen, Fujian, PRC

Zhuhai Development SEZ
Shuiwantou
Guangdong Province, PRC

Travel Services

American Express
L115D China World Trade
Center Arcade
1 Jian Guo Hen Waida Jie
Beijing, PRC
Tel: (1) 505-2639, 4406, 7

American Express
Unit 221-222, the Mall
Pacific Place
88 Queensway
Hong Kong
Tel: 844021

China International Travel Svc.
60 East 42nd St.—Suite 465
New, York, NY 10165
(212) 867-0271

China National Tourist Office
333 West Broadway—Suite 201
Glendale, CA 91204
(818) 545-7505

China Travel Service (H.K.)
CTS House, 4/F
72-83 Connaught Road
Central Hong Kong
Tel: 853-3533

U.S.-China Travel Service
119 S. Atlantic Blvd.—Ste #303
U.S. CTS Building
Monterey Park, CA 91754
(818) 457-8668

American Express
New World Tower Bldg. G/F
16-18 Queen's Road Central
Hong Kong
Tel: 8448668

American Express
Shops 9 & 10, 1st/Floor
111-139 Nathan Rd.
Kowloon, Hong Kong
Tel: 7391386

American Express
Park Lane Radisson Hotel
310 Gloucester Rd.
Causeway Bay, Hong Kong
Tel: 8393640

U.S. China Travel Service
2/F 212 Sutter Street
San Francisco, CA 94108
(415) 398-6627

China Travel Service (H.K.)
1/F, Alpha House
27-33 Nathan Road
Kowloon, Hong Kong
Tel: 721-1331

China Travel Service (H.K.)
2/F, China Travel Building
77 Queen's Road
Central Hong Kong
Tel: 525-2284

U.S. Embassy and Consulates in China

Embassy of the United States
of America
3 Xiushui Beijie
Beijing, PRC
Tel: 532-1831

U.S. Consul-General
1469 Huai Hai Zhong Lu
Shanghai 200031, PRC
Tel: (86-21) 433-6880

U.S. Consul-General
40 Lane 4, Sec. 5
Sanjing St., Heping, PRC
Tel: 290000

U.S. Consul-General
1 Shamain South Street
Guangzhou, Guangdong, PRC
Tel: (86-20) 888-8911

U.S. Consul-General
Jinjiang Hotel
36 Renmin Nan Rd.
Chengdu, PRC
Tel: 51912

U.S. Consul-General
26 Garden Road
Central Hong Kong
Tel: 239011

U.S. Government Agencies

Agency for International
Development
320 21st St. NW
Washington, D.C. 20523
(202) 663-1451

Department of Agriculture
ERS-China Section
1301 New York Ave. NW #264
Washington, D.C. 20005-4788
(202) 219-0625

Office of PRC & Hong Kong
US Department of Commerce
14th St. & Constitution Ave.#2317
Washington, D.C. 20230
(202) 482-3583

U.S. Department of State
East Asian Affairs
Washington, D.C. 20520
(202) 647-2538
(202) 647-6300

Far East Law Division
Library of Congress
Washington, D.C. 20540
(202) 287-5085

International Trade Admin.
14th and Constitution Aves.
Washington, D.C. 20230
(202) 377-2000

Overseas Private Investment
Corp.
1615 M Street NW
Washington, D.C. 20527
(202) 457-7200

Small Business Administration
Office of International Trade
1441 L Street
Washington, D.C. 20416
(202) 634-1500

14. Additional Reading

Abend, Hallet Edward. *Treaty Ports*. Garden City, New York: Doubleday, 1944. (A history of treaties and treaty ports in China.)

American Chamber of Commerce. *Living in Hong Kong*. (8th ed.) Hong Kong: American Chamber of Commerce in Hong Kong, 1992. (A detailed guide covering everything from the move to Hong Kong to housing, health, schools, transport.)

Chu, Godwin C. and Ju, Yanan. *The Great Wall in Ruins: Communication and Cultural Change in China*. Albany, New York: State University of New York Press, 1993.

Des Forges, Roger V., Luo Ning, and Wu Yen-bo (ed.). *Chinese Democracy and the Crisis of 1989*. Albany, New York: State University of New York, 1993. (An analysis of China's political and social crises in the 1980s).

Department of Commerce. *Doing Business with China*. Washington, D.C.: U.S. Department of Commerce, 1988. (Good but old.)

Fairbank, John King. *China: A New History*. Boston: Harvard University Press, 1993. (A great scholar's last book, based on recent research.)

Forestier, Katherine. *The Hong Kong Connection—Doing Business in Guangdong Province*. Hong Kong: American Chamber of Commerce in Hong Kong, 1989. (Describes in detail important aspects of establishing a business in Guangdong Province.)

Hu Wenzhong and Grove, Cornelius L. *Encountering the Chinese: A Guide for Americans*. Yarmouth, ME: Intercultural Press, 1991. (A sensitive cross-cultural analysis.)

Jackson, Sukhan. *Chinese Enterprise Management*. Berlin: de Gruyter and Co., 1992. (An inside view of Chinese management.)

Kalb, Rosalind, and Welch, Penelope. *Moving Your Family Overseas*. Yarmouth, ME: Intercultural Press, 1992. (A step-by-step guide for moving abroad.)

MacLeod, Roderick K. *China, Inc.: How to Do Business with the Chinese*. New York: Bantam Books, 1988. (Useful but dated.)

Terry, Edith. *The Executive Guide to China*. New York: John Wiley and Sons, 1984. (Excellent coverage of the details involving planning, organizing, and conducting a business trip to China.)

Xue Muqiao. *China's Socialist Economy*. Beijing: Foreign Language Press, 1986. (Good coverage of reforms in pricing and wages.)

Zee, A. *Swallowing Clouds*. New York: Simon and Schuster, 1990. (Analysis of the nexus between Chinese language and cuisine.)

SPECIAL ECONOMIC ZONES

Qinhuangdao

Tianjin

Dalian

Yantai

Qingdao

Lianyungang

Open Areas Surround:

Guangzhou
Xiamen
Shanghai-Nantong
Yantai-Quingdao
Dalian

Nantong

Shanghai

Ningbo

Wenzhou

Fuzhou

Xiamen

Taiwan

Shantou

Guangzhou

Shenzhen

Zhuhai

Hong Kong

Beihai

Zhanjiang

KEY

☐ Special Economic Zones (5)

⬤ Open Cities (14)

Hainan

Index

0251